A Devotional

First
Love

Romancing His Bride
Responding as His Bride

"My beloved is mine and I am His"
Song of Songs 2:16

Nancy M. Wilson

A profound mystery of love . . .

And you husbands must love your wives with the same love
Christ showed the church. He gave up His life for her to make her
holy and clean, washed by baptism and God's Word. He did this
to present her to Himself as a glorious church without a spot or
wrinkle or any other blemish. Instead, she will be holy and
without fault. In the same way, husbands ought to love their
wives as they love their own bodies.
Ephesians 5:25-28

Let us rejoice and be glad and give Him glory! For the wedding of the
Lamb has come, and His bride has made herself ready.
Revelation 19:7 NIV

First Love: Romancing His Bride & Responding as His Bride
By Nancy M. Wilson with selected poems by Jack Wilson

Copyright © 2000 by Venture Media

Cover and interior design by Sally Brown.

ISBN 1-56399-156-X

Printed in the United States of America

Dedications

To Mom and Dad

Your steadfast love and godly example for the past 50 years have graced our family with a treasured heritage. [Mom and Dad] You have modeled this covenant love, and have left a legacy to six children and twelve grandchildren who love you dearly.

To My Ministry Partners

Thank you for loving me and Jesus Christ, our Lord, during these past 25 years in the service of our King! You have been a part of all He has done.

To My Beloved King and Bridegroom

You made the dream of this book a reality. I offer myself afresh to You—to love, glorify and fulfill Your purposes in my life; awaiting the day I will be united with You for all eternity.

All the good things I have are from You. You will show me the way of life, granting me the joy of Your presence and the pleasures of living with You forever.
Psalm 16:2b, 11

Table of Contents

Romancing His Bride

Responding as a Bride

In Acknowledgement

My special thanks to several friends, who generously shared their gifts to make this vision a reality…

- Sally Brown, whose creative design gifts grace this book with elegance.

- Patty McClung (my angel), who amazed me with her giving heart to type, edit and offer invaluable advice; doing what ever it took to get the job done.

- Melanie Wilson (my dear sister-in-law), who graciously edited and added her expertise.

- Kathy Corpus, Dolores Livingstone, Lee Ferchaud and Dan Lee, who prayed and helped edit.

- Sandy & Pearl, my prayer partners, who made publishing possible! Along with many others who make up my ministry team, and have blessed me through their friendship, prayers and support these past 25 years.

- Erik Segalini, Paul Roberts & Geoffrey Harris, whose professional counsel helped me so much.

To God be all the glory!

And this same God who takes care of me will supply all your needs from His glorious riches, which have been given to us in Christ Jesus. Now glory be to God our Father forever and ever. Amen.
Philippians 4:19-20

Introduction

Perhaps there's a part of all of us that wants to experience a fairy tale romance—to know pure love that lifts us out of ourselves into the ecstasy of being desired and cherished by someone who has captured our heart. We are not satisfied with fairy tales, though; we desire the real thing. In this devotional you will find a collection of love poems and parallels of divine love—the love of a bridegroom for his bride, and the love of our heavenly Bridegroom for all of us, His beloved bride (the church). This is no fairy tale—it is a love story in the purest sense. Ephesians 1:4 assures us that we were "chosen before the creation of the world" to share this eternal love relationship. It is this picture of love that has won the hearts of all who make up the bride of Jesus Christ, the Lamb of God.

I have been privileged to observe the love of my father and mother, which began 50 years ago. Over the years, I've discovered a treasure of love poems that began their precious romance that continues to this day. Dad will be the first to say his is a human, imperfect love; and yet, I might add a God-given love inspired by a divine Lover.

Part I, Romancing His Bride, contains 25 of Dad's many love poems, and brings to life his passionate love for his bride. As Dad wooed his bride, won her heart, and wonderfully loved and cared for her, may you find your heart being romanced by your heavenly Bridegroom.

God's Word is His love letter to you. I pray the parallels will bless you with an ever increasing awareness of the Lover of your soul, and will encourage you in your love relationships here on earth.

Throughout the devotional, I have woven in the rich symbolism of a traditional Jewish betrothal and marriage celebration to show how clearly it foreshadows Jesus Christ purchasing His beloved bride. I trust these insights will bring new meaning to every aspect of human and divine romance.

What fun it's been to reminisce with Mom and Dad about their romance...

The year was 1947. Dad had recently returned from three years in the

Air Force. He was now completing college at St. Louis University. Dad played football throughout high school and played minor league baseball for the St. Louis Browns. He was actually quite a star athlete. I found lots of newspaper clippings about Jack Wilson, my dad. Not only was he in great physical shape, but he was one handsome guy! He was an ambitious, hard-working, intelligent young man who had lots of hope for his future.

Mom was working for the government. She enjoyed socializing with her girlfriends and had several young men pursuing her. She possessed a sweet, fun-loving personality along with a natural charm and beauty.

The "Ice Breaker" dance was a night not to be forgotten. LaVerne and Jack both had tons of friends. He came with his buddies, and she with her girlfriends.

Dad recounts the evening he met Mom as "history." LaVerne Rose Knobbe caught his eye. He asked for a dance. Never one to be indecisive or slow, he probably had a confident, humorous and romantic style of courting Mom.

For the next three years, while Dad finished college, he pursued and won his bride. Poems flowed from his pen with ease. He wrote most of them while in class; it's amazing he passed. He presented them personally and through special delivery. Mom treasured and kept them in a special memory box containing pictures and reminders of their love.

Finally, after three years of laying a solid foundation of love and friendship, Dad proposed at a romantic dinner-dance where they were surrounded by a bounty of friends with whom to celebrate.

On August 19, 1950, they sealed their commitment in the covenant of marriage— "for better or for worse, 'til death do us part."

Fifty years later, Mom and Dad share a precious love and devotion to one another. I've witnessed an intimate love blossoming into a daily partnership and companionship. Over the years they have been blessed with six children and twelve grandchildren who have been the recipients of their sacrificial love. Through happiness and sadness, delightful and tough times, their love has been solid, because it's been based on the Lover of their Souls, the Rock of Ages, Jesus Christ.

For many years, Mom and Dad played tennis and golfed together, enjoyed many rich friendships, struggled and worked together to support a large family, while honoring God in it all. Now they are facing a new season of challenge. Mom has been diagnosed with Alzheimer's disease and cannot respond in the same way. How beautiful it is to witness Dad's steadfast love for Mom now, and to see the fire of his devotion still burning.

Part II, Responding as His Bride, will allow you to go further in your understanding of what it means to be the bride of Jesus Christ.

"First love" can be intoxicating. The eye of the lover is solely focused on the beloved, so that nothing else really matters in light of this new romance. Present and future dreams revolve around the beloved—everything is affected by this intense love and passion.

But what about after the honeymoon? How can you keep the fire burning and the fresh passion of "first love" alive? Any marriage is in danger of deteriorating if it's not nurtured and cultivated. In a similar way, our relationship with our divine Lover needs to grow and develop. We are warned in Revelation 2:4 about losing our "first love." We should guard against taking our love relationship for granted. The solution is given in Revelation 2:5 to "remember the height from which you have fallen! Repent and do the things you did at first." Remember that extra effort you gave to win your sweetheart's affection when you were dating? Well, you need to admit that recently you've been neglectful; then—start doing, again, what you did in the beginning!

My 25 poems are but a meager response to my Beloved's love for me. My poetry is written testimony to my intimate relationship with the

Bridegroom of my soul. I humbly share them with you as a love gift back to my Savior, Prince, and Bridegroom—the "fairest of the sons of men," (Psalm 45:2, RSV), who has captured my heart and become the love of my life. I pray He will ravish your heart as He has mine.

I can vividly remember when my love relationship with Jesus Christ began. Ever since I was a little girl, I knew about Him. I grew up with parents who talked about Him and took me to church. But somehow, as I grew up, I knew I was missing something. It was the difference between knowing about someone and really "knowing" him. My search for satisfaction and significance led me to look for false substitutes. Guys, parties, popularity, and success didn't fulfill my heart's deepest need. In fact, I became disillusioned and empty; I found myself struggling with a serious eating disorder. One Sunday in church with a hangover, I told God I didn't want to be a hypocrite and I left. I asked Him to reveal Himself to me in a personal way if He was real and could help me.

Amazing things began to happen. I met several Christian guys and a Gideon gave me a Bible that I immediately began to read. But it was at a party in my dorm one memorable evening that I heard the greatest love story I've ever known: "For God so loved the world that He gave His one and only Son, that whoever believes in him shall not perish but have eternal life." (John 3:16 NIV) My eyes and heart were opened in a new way as I saw my need for Jesus. The thought of His unconditional, sacrificial love for me, and His willingness to give His life in exchange for mine was overwhelming. I was worth so much to Him that He had purchased me with His own blood.

A fresh understanding gripped my heart; big tears rolled down my cheeks as I prayed and opened my heart to receive His undeserved love and forgiveness. Joy flooded my soul and peace calmed my restless heart knowing I had been delivered from the power of sin in my life. "So if the Son sets you free, you will be free indeed." (John 8:36)

Not only did I experience a new freedom and hope for my future, but also a consuming passion to know Jesus better. Our intimate relationship began on March 15, 1972. Like any growing relationship, there have been ups and downs—both ecstasy and discouragement. But His faithful, committed love for me has drawn me into an ever-deepening passion for Him. He alone can satisfy and quench the longing in my heart. I have never known the love of an earthly Bridegroom, but I have been smitten by the love of the Prince of Peace and the King of Kings.

The greatest truth I carry in my heart is that He's preparing me for the day I will be with Him for all eternity. Until then, He has graciously called me to serve Him in full-time ministry. In partnership with my Bridegroom, I've had the privilege of serving with Campus Crusade for Christ for the past 25 years—a journey that began August 6, 1975. He's sent me all over His world to share the gospel and mobilize youth and leaders to help fulfill the Great Commission in this generation.

My primary mission is to respond as the bride of Jesus Christ by loving and glorifying Him. Please join me in being romanced as His bride and responding as His Bride. It is my prayer that as you spend these moments reflecting upon your "first love," you will respond as a bride to the Lover of your soul. May you be inspired and encouraged on your journey to His heart.

Nancy,
Beloved Bride of Jesus Christ

Responding as His Bride

Someday

Because you mean so much to me
our Natures' part will play
Her role of ever righteousness
and make you mine someday
I pledge to you my loyalty
and place my trust in you
And promise I will be the man
that you expect me to
There'd be no more that I could ask
no part of earthliness
Could gain me any favor more
if you I could possess
It's only you for whom I live
my thoughts and every deed
Can only be complete for me
if they can fill your need
And all the stars that ever shine
and rolling clouds above
Can only know the fervor of
my everlasting love

Jack Wilson
June 21, 1948

Long ago the LORD said to Israel: "I have loved you, My people with an everlasting love. With unfailing love I have drawn you to Myself."
⌢Jeremiah 31:3⌢

To be the object of someone's love and affection is the cry of our heart. We all long to be chosen as a special, unique and treasured person. My father fell in love with my mother and wrote about his dream of "someday" being the man who could claim her as his bride. With the passion of his devotion, he pursued her love in response.

Dad was persistent in his pursuit of Mom. He was creative in courting her, and always tried to look his best when he left his father's house. However, matching clothes was never his strength. On one occasion, Mom sent him home to change clothes. Not easily discouraged, he kept coming until finally three years later, he would claim Mom's hand in marriage.

How similar to the traditional Jewish marriage wherein the prospective bridegroom took the initiative and traveled from his father's house to woo his bride. It was his father's goal to find a bride for his son.

Christ also left His Father's house and came to earth to gain a bride for Himself. "How we praise God, the Father of our Lord Jesus Christ, Who has blessed us with every spiritual blessing in the heavenly realms because we belong to Christ. Long ago, even before He made the world, God loved us and chose us in Christ to be holy and without fault in His eyes. His unchanging plan has always been to adopt us into His own family by bringing us to Himself through Jesus Christ. And this gave Him great pleasure. So we praise God for the wonderful kindness He has poured out on us because we belong to His dearly loved Son." (Ephesians 1:3-6)

Because of our union with Jesus, our Bridegroom, we are adopted into the family of God. We have royal blood and an eternal inheritance! You were chosen before the creation of the world. He saw you, imperfections and all, and set His love upon you, desiring you to be His very own. Winning your love was the reason He came. Have you accepted the Father's love gift of salvation through His Son Jesus?

I Pledge Myself

You are the whole of life to me
your each component part
is the essence of the girl
I've taken in my heart
I love you for the many ways
that you have bettered me
Your every act and deed has been
of finer quality
In every way you stand above
and hold the highest place
You are the only one my heart
forever will embrace
I pledge my life to serving you
in bondage I will be
And I would will it all my life
and through eternity
So darling let me say the words
I'll need not to rehearse
"forever will you be my wife
for better or for worse."

JW

I created you and have cared for you since you were born. I will be your
God through all your lifetime, yes, even when your hair is white with
age. I made you and I will care for you. I will carry you
along and be your Savior.
Isaiah 46:3-4 TLB

y father pledged his love and devotion to my mother forever—for better or for worse. He praised her and acknowledged her worth and value. She alone held the highest place in his heart. He didn't know what the future would hold, He only knew who held the future. So he made a commitment to love and serve my mother in the covenant of marriage, " 'til death do us part."

In the Jewish wedding tradition, the father of the prospective bride negotiated with the prospective bridegroom the price that must be paid to purchase his bride. Jesus Christ paid to purchase us with His own blood. "For you know that it was not with perishable things such as silver or gold that you were redeemed from the empty way of life handed down to you from your forefathers, but with the precious blood of Christ, a lamb without blemish or defect." (1 Peter 1:18-19 NIV)

He has pledged Himself to you forever if you choose Him as your Savior and Bridegroom. Pledge yourself to Him as His bride by responding to His love and sacrifice. In return, He promises, "Never will I leave you; never will I forsake you." (Hebrews 13:5b NIV)

Faith Alone

No one could ever mean as much
or ever take your place
Your loving arms are mine alone
your every fond embrace
My heart has no intention of
forgetting you are part
of the every thought and deed
that dwell within my heart
But love is based on truthfulness
and that I've always found
is the only reason that
I'll ever be around
My faith in you is endless and
no doubts I've ever known
It's meaningless to say how much
my love for you has grown
But if someone could ever give
to you much more than I
Because I love you dearly I
would part and say goodbye

JW
July 12, 1948

Can a mother forget the baby at her breast and have no compassion on the child she has borne? Though she may forget, I will not forget you! See, I have engraved you on the palms of My hands.
⌐Isaiah 49:15-16a NIV⌐

*M*y father promised that he had no intention of forgetting my mother. He told her that his thoughts were always of her and that no one could take her place. Your Bridegroom also loves you with an intense and personal love. No one can take your place. He is thinking about you constantly.

He has had you in His heart since before you were formed in your mother's womb. You are His delightful masterpiece. So mindful is He of you, that He has engraved your name on the palms of His hands.

You have probably had the experience of being rejected or abandoned by someone you loved. Overcoming the pain inflicted by these experiences can be difficult. How wonderful it is to know that you have a Friend, a Parent, and a Lover who will never leave you.

Have you contemplated this commitment your Bridegroom has to you? Why not embrace His faith in you by placing more of your faith in Him alone?

You Are My Tenant

If all the hours that we shared
were totaled for their worth
I would show you what I meant
by heaven here on earth
I love you as the day is long
and if wishing could increase
The hours that we spent would be
subjected to a lease
I'd make you sign a contract for
your lifetime and a day
And there would be a clause that you
would never go away
You'd be my only tenant and
my only property
And darling I would prove to you
how faithful I could be
I'd be the landlord of your life
and my only fee
Would be for you to whisper that
you are in love with me
So if sometime I can employ
some magic over you
I'll build a castle in the clouds
the day you say, "I do"

JW
October 13, 1948

Or don't you know that your body is the temple of the Holy Spirit,
who lives in you and was given to you by God? You do not belong to
yourself, for God bought you with a high price. So you
must honor God with your body.

1 Corinthians 6:19-20

My father's analogy of wanting to be the landlord of Mom's life is so precious! God has also given us an endearing analogy calling us the temple of His Holy Spirit. As we begin a relationship with Jesus, He gives us His Holy Spirit to indwell us and live through us. We are His precious possession.

When the Jewish bridegroom paid the purchase price for his bride, the marriage covenant was established. At that point, the man and woman were regarded as husband and wife even though no physical union had taken place. In a similar way, the Church, the collective body of Christ, has been declared sanctified, or set apart, exclusively for Christ. We have been sealed by the Holy Spirit as God's possession. Ephesians 1:13b-14 explains, "Having believed, you were marked in Him with a seal, the promised Holy Spirit, who is a deposit guaranteeing our inheritance until the redemption of those who are God's possession—to the praise of His glory." (NIV)

Is He the tenant of your heart? Have you allowed the Holy Spirit to fill and control you—to be the landlord of your life? Tell Him of your desire now. He wants to prove His faithful love to you and possess you fully.

You Are My Life

I look at you with longing pride
within my heart I find
A love so fervent that you are
forever on my mind
Because my darling you impress
me with your every smile
Though life consists of only time
I'll love you all the while
You are my living doll and
on every single day
I discover what it means
to love you in this way
It's given me a brighter path
a goal I can attain
If always I possess you and
with me you will remain
And I will always be as true
as you have ever been
And with your love you've made of me
the happiest of men
Lover

JW
≈July 29, 1948≈

On the night when He was betrayed, the Lord Jesus took a loaf of bread,
and when He had given thanks, He broke it and said, "This is My body,
which is given for you. Do this in remembrance of Me." In the same
way, He took the cup of wine after supper saying, "This cup is the new
covenant between God and you, sealed by the shedding of My blood.
Do this in remembrance of Me as often as you drink it."
1 Corinthians 11:23b-25

Marriage involves a complete giving of oneself. My father discovered a passionate love that compelled him to want to give of himself completely to my mother. This was his focus and goal. The Jewish groom and bride drank from a cup over which the betrothal benediction was pronounced. This act symbolized that the covenant relationship had been established.

Jesus Christ demonstrated His covenant love at the Last Supper. As He prepared to offer His body and blood on the cross, He pronounced His covenant love for His bride. Every time we partake of communion we are symbolically saying, "I do" desire to be fully united with my sacrificial Lover. As we partake of His body and blood in communion, we look forward in anticipation of our final union for all eternity, the wedding feast of the Lamb. What a goal to live for!

Just as a bride and bridegroom direct all their energy toward their relationship, let all your thoughts and desires revolve around your union with Christ now and forever. Each day, pray for new insights into His intimate love for you, and new ways to demonstrate your devotion to Him.

Forever and a Day

Though miles have taken you from me
and left us far apart
You live within me spiritually
forever near my heart
Distance is a milestone that
is overcome by will
I know I'll always love you and
you are my greatest thrill
My dreams alone are mine to share
whatever thoughts they may
You are the only dream I hold
forever and a day
So with these calculations I
implore you to recall
That hours new are yet to come
however large or small

JW

*"But when the Holy Spirit has come upon you, you will receive power
and will tell people about me everywhere—in Jerusalem, throughout
Judea, in Samaria, and to the ends of the earth." It was not long after
He said this that He was taken up into the sky while they were watching,
and He disappeared into a cloud. As they were straining their eyes to
see Him, two white-robed men suddenly stood there among them. They
said, "Men of Galilee, why are you standing here staring at the sky?
Jesus has been taken away from you into heaven. And someday,
just as you saw Him go, He will return!"*

☞ *Acts 1:8-11* ☜

While playing minor league baseball, Dad was temporarily separated from my mother. I imagine that thinking of her helped him win a few more games! Distance did not change his love and commitment to her. With anticipation, he asked her to recall hours yet to come when they would be reunited again.

The Jewish bridegroom left the home of his bride after the marriage covenant was in effect and returned to his father's house. Christ, our Bridegroom, returned to His Father's house following the payment of His purchase price. The price was His precious life poured out for His bride so He could redeem her forever.

Imagine the disciples watching the risen Lord Jesus ascend into heaven. With mixed emotions they realized He had left them. His indwelling Holy Spirit was promised to empower them as His witnesses to the very ends of the earth. As they strained to see a last glimpse of Him, they were assured of His return.

Think of the hours yet ahead when He will come again for you. Hide this truth in your heart as a treasure when you are tempted to give in to loneliness, sadness, or despair. Let His Holy Spirit give you the power of hope for today and forever. Then, as we wait to be united with our Bridegroom, we can tell others of the wonders of His love.

My Queen Forever

I would be a king if you'd
consent to be my queen
And our castle would enfold
the things that I've foreseen
There would be a servant for
your every one command
And I'd instruct my subjects to
obey your each demand
I'd fill your room with roses and
along your path I'd strew
Gardenias rare to only prove
my deepest love for you
But darling I'd be happy just
to manifest my love
For someone who's as sweet as you
I'm always thinking of
And when my castle in the sky
is ready for you, Dear
I hope that you'll consent to be
my queen for every year.

JW

Don't be troubled. You trust God, now trust in Me. There are many rooms in My Father's home, and I am going to prepare a place for you. If this were not so, I would tell you plainly. When everything is ready, I will come and get you, so that you will always be with Me where I am.

John 14:1-3

*M*y father must have wondered how his lover would respond. Would she consent to be his queen? Would she be eager to prepare for their future together? Theirs was not an arranged marriage; she was free to choose. We are also free to choose Jesus as our King and His kingdom as our destination now and eternally.

At traditional Jewish weddings, the bridegroom is considered a king, and his bride, his queen. As the bride of Messiah—a bride comprised of men, women, and children— we have a Bridegroom who is a King. He left this earth to prepare a place for us in His eternal kingdom.

It cost Jesus a great deal to purchase us as His bride. As He was being questioned by Pilate during His trial before going to the cross, He was asked by Pilate, "You are a king then?" Yeshua (Hebrew name for Jesus) answered, "My kingdom is not of the world. You are right in saying I am a king, and for this I came into the world, to testify to the truth." (John 18: 36a, 37b NIV)

Jesus came into the world to purchase His bride and set up His eternal kingdom. Will you choose His lordship as your King and Lover? He is King and desires to possess you completely. This comes from your glad surrender of your heart to His intimate love and purpose for your life. Will you bow your heart before Yeshua the King today? He is the King of kings and Lord of lords, and He wants to give you the kingdom! Can you imagine that?!

Love Has No Words

Darling I can find no way
To tell you how I feel
I never knew that love could be
So genuine and real
If words could fit together to
Express my love for you
There would be no truer things
That I could say or do
but all the many thoughts of you
That Blossom from my heart
Do not seem to come to me
except when we're apart
so whenever you are with me, Dear
It's meaningless to say
All the little things to you
I'd like to tell each day
I save up all my memories
And all my dreams of you
To keep them for a rainy day
When I get feeling blue
Then the cloudy skies above
go passing on their way
The birds are winging through the air
And I am feeling gay.

JW

How precious are Your thoughts about me, O God! They are
innumerable! I can't even count them; they outnumber the grains of
sand! And when I wake up in the morning, You are still with me!
Psalm 139:17, 18

y father's genuine love for his bride portrays just a fraction of our Bridegroom's love for us. He has us in His heart and is constantly thinking of us. Dad found joy in memories of Mom and delighted in those thoughts when cloudy skies came his way.

To be known completely with an intimate awareness of one's thoughts, feelings and motives is what pure love must be based upon. Otherwise, love would falter when imperfection is discovered. How incredible that God has an intimate knowledge of us combined with an intense love for us.

Have you grasped the fact that you bring joy to the heart of God? Your unique personality, makeup, and temperament are known and cherished by Him. Revel in this thought today, for love has no words to compare with His word: "The LORD your God is with you, He is mighty to save. He will take great delight in you, He will quiet you with His love, He will rejoice over you with singing." (Zephaniah 3:17, NIV)

How I Feel

It's wonderful to know my friends
without dissent agree
that you are all the many things
that I had said you'd be
I reminded them of all
your many qualities
and told them that without a doubt
with you they would be pleased
And darling each and every one
agrees wholeheartedly
that you were even more than I
predicted you would be
And though I do appreciate
their kind regard of you
I can express my feelings in
a simple phrase or two
I love you darling of my dreams
and Sweetheart of my life
I want you to consent to be
my ever loving wife.

JW

O My beloved, you are as beautiful as the lovely town of Tirzah.
Yes, as beautiful as Jerusalem! You are as majestic as an army with
banners! Look away, for your eyes overcome me! Your hair falls in
waves, like a flock of goats frisking down the slopes of Gilead. Your
teeth are as white as newly washed sheep. They are perfectly matched;
not one is missing. Your cheeks behind your veil are like pomegranate
halves—lovely and delicious. There may be sixty wives, all queens,
and eighty concubines and unnumbered virgins available to me.
But I would still choose my dove, my perfect one, the only beloved
daughter of her mother! The young women are delighted when
they see her; even queens and concubines sing her praises!
Song of Songs 6:4-9

It is said, "beauty is in the eye of the beholder." King Solomon gives us a glimpse of his passionate love for his bride. She is unique and "perfect" in his eyes. Dad describes his delight in the approval of his friends for his bride. They acknowledge her beauty and qualities worth praising.

When the time arrives for the long-awaited wedding celebration, a Jewish bridegroom will conduct a torchlight procession to the home of his bride with his best man and male escorts. They will all share in the joy of their love and union.

John records, "a bridegroom's friend rejoices with him." (John 3:29)

When our heavenly Bridegroom comes from His Father's house in heaven, He will come accompanied by an angelic host to take His bride to her eternal home. Are your friends ready to celebrate with you? Have you shared your Bridegroom's love with them? You may be the one to introduce them to Jesus.

Be My Valentine

Once a year there comes a day
when I am free to choose
The girl I've set my heart on
and then I break the news
By sending her a Valentine
bright red and trimmed with lace
That only is a token of
her beauty and her grace
But I can never hope to match
the blueness of your eyes
That hold the warmth of springtime
and reflect the fairest skies
A smile that seems to penetrate
the caverns of my heart
That always hold you close to me
whenever we're apart
Because you are the little girl
that God has given me
Like an angel from above
that sets my heart afree
I know I'll always want you, Dear,
to hold you close as mine
And through the years
You'll always be
My ONLY Valentine
Jack

JW
1949

God showed how much He loved us by sending His only Son into the world so that we might have eternal life through Him. This is real love. It is not that we loved God, but that He loved us and sent His Son as a sacrifice to take away our sins.

1 John 4:9-10

*D*ad was a creative lover. I've seen some of his beautiful Valentines saved in Mom's treasure box. He treasured her as a gift from God. She had captivated him and he set his heart on obtaining her love.

God sent a personalized Valentine to you. It was wrapped in human flesh and trimmed with divinity. Crimson red was the cost of His sacrifice given to you. He saw you in beauty and grace—a reflection of His own image. "God saved you by His special favor when you believed. And you can't take credit for this; it is a gift from God. Salvation is not a reward for the good things we have done, so none of us can boast about it. For we are God's masterpiece. He has created us anew in Christ Jesus, so that we can do the good things He planned for us long ago." (Ephesians 2:8-10)

You are God's masterpiece—His poem written before the world was formed. His invitation is given to "Be My Valentine" for all eternity. "And this is the testimony: God has given us eternal life, and this life is in His Son. He who has the Son has life; he who does not have the Son of God does not have life." (1 John 5:11-12 NIV)

Will you be His valentine? Express your love and gratitude for His expensive gift to purchase you. Place your confidence solely in Jesus, your eternal Valentine.

My Dreams Are You

There is a little world that I
can safely call my own
Because the sole inhabitants
are you and I alone
But though a dreamland it might be
a figment of my mind
I know that it cannot escape
and happiness I'll find
For though I face reality
as little as I may
My dreams of you will always turn
the darkest night to day
Because your smile has opened all
the dreams within my heart
I find it no illusion that
we're never far apart.
Love, Jack

JW

For the Lord Himself will come down from heaven with a commanding shout, with the call of the archangel, and with the trumpet call of God. First, all the Christians who have died will rise from their graves. Then, together with them, we who are still alive and remain on the earth will be caught up in the clouds to meet the Lord in the air and remain with Him forever.
1 Thessalonians 4:16-17

Every bride longs for her wedding day. She dreams of the day when finally her preparations will be complete and her bridegroom will be hers forever. In my dad's expression of longing, we see a glimpse of the Bridegroom's eager anticipation. Though a Jewish bride didn't know the exact time her groom would come for her, she knew his coming was preceded by a shout.

Christ's return will also be accompanied by the voice of the archangel and the trumpet call of God. It's as if all heaven has been preparing for the grand event. The waiting will end and God's trumpet will announce the royal Bridegroom coming for His bride. For all eternity, His dreams have been for His eternal companion, the bride of Christ.

This is no dream, but the reality of one day meeting the Lord face-to-face. He is our King and Bridegroom forever and we will rule and reign with Him in His ever-expanding kingdom. Let your imigination run wild—day-dreaming about His soon return! Maranatha! Lord, come quickly!

Your Name Means Everything

To gaze into the chasm of
your eyes so very blue
Restraint is not to keep me from
confessing "I love you"
The ladder of success is high
its steps a journey long
With thoughts of you to guide me I
can climb it with a song
You make my life so wonderful
and everything I do
Could never mean a thing to me
unless it were for you
A name is just a symbol and
it designates no worth
But your name means more to me
than anything on earth
You are so beautiful to me
the fortune in my life
And my ship will land ashore
the day we're man and wife
Jack

JW
no date

Look, I am coming quickly. Hold on to what you have, so that no one will take away your crown. All who are victorious will become pillars in the temple of my God, and they will never have to leave it. And I will write My God's name on them, and they will be citizens in the city of My God—the new Jerusalem that comes down from heaven from My God. And they will have My new name inscribed upon them. Anyone who is willing to hear should listen to the Spirit and understand what the Spirit is saying to the churches.

Revelation 3:11-13

*M*y father's ardent longing to honor my mother is a glimpse of what God desires for those who know and love Him.

Jesus, our Bridegroom, is awaiting the day He will come for His beloved bride. He wants to find His bride expectantly waiting, anticipating His return. Though He longs for this day, He knows that there will be a time of testing and suffering before He comes. With His strong love and the power of His shed blood, His bride can overcome. "Remain faithful even when facing death, and I will give you the crown of life." (Revelation 2:10)

There are so many treasures and rewards He has stored up for those who belong to Him and have learned the secret of bridal love. Jesus is a Bridegroom who treasures His bride. With great affection, He has chosen a new name for each of us who make up the bridal host. Your name means everything to Him. Listen closely today and hear Him gently call your name.

Only You Alone

My love is like an ember and
forever will retain
Its fervent warmth and place for you
so long as I remain
Because there never has nor will
there be a single day
That I can't point with pride and know
you've helped me in some way
For you and only you alone
I'd ever compromise
Because I know I love you when
I gaze into your eyes
Their warmth and kindness like a hand
reach out and tenderly
Bring a wealth of happiness
and sing their song to me
So since the very day that we
were brought together, Dear
I know that I have wanted you
on every day each year.
Jack

~JW~

Then I heard again what sounded like the shout of a huge crowd, or the roar of mighty ocean waves, or the crash of loud thunder: "Hallelujah! For the Lord our God, the Almighty, reigns. Let us be glad and rejoice and honor Him. For the time has come for the wedding feast of the Lamb, and His bride has prepared herself. She is permitted to wear the finest white linen." (Fine linen represents the good deeds done by the people of God.)
⌒Revelation 19:6-8⌒

*F*rom the day my father and mother were brought together, his love was kindled like an ember. There was a place in his heart only for her. A bridegroom has eyes only for his bride. He longs for her, desiring to be fully united in the consummation of their marriage.

Finally, the wedding day has arrived! The climax of all history culminates in this glorious event. The bride has been prepared through the waiting and refining process. She has made herself ready as she has yielded her will and become one in purpose with her Bridegroom. All over the world, those who love Jesus are preparing themselves, as collectively they will make up the bride of Jesus Christ. Many have suffered greatly and have "washed their robes in the blood of the Lamb and made them white." (Revelation 7:14b) She is now clothed in her pure white linen bridal gown, signifying the righteousness Jesus has bestowed upon her.

When the day arrives for a traditional Jewish wedding, the bride and groom enter the bridal chamber and in the privacy of that place, they consummate their marriage. One day in heaven, Christ's union with the church will take place for all eternity. Let us rejoice and be glad as we prepare for our eternal wedding day!

Easter Day

On this Easter day to you
I send this message, Dear
That you have given me new hope
whenever you were near
The sun is always shining and
my days are always bright
Only when you part from me
the sunshine fades to night
To when we promenade this morn
the sweetness you enfold
Will capture all the fairness that
this earthly world can hold
You'll wear a bonnet on your hair
its grace imparts to you
All the fairness of the sky
and of the morning's dew
So as the years go fleeting by
forever I'll be gay
If I know you'll love me, Dear
on every Easter day.

JW
1949

I am overwhelmed with joy in the LORD my God! For He has
dressed me with the clothing of salvation and draped me in a robe
of righteousness. I am like a bridegroom in his wedding suit or
a bride with her jewels.
Isaiah 61:10

Your bridegroom is a King who wants to display the beauty of His bride. Just as my father found both joy and hope in the presence of his bride, so does our heavenly Bridegroom. You are adorned in righteousness, and covered with grace. What an exquisite wardrobe—purchased at great price—by your royal Husband!

Every day can be Easter for the bride of Jesus Christ. For our Bridegroom furnishes the most beautiful garments of salvation fresh and clean, free from spot or stain. The robe of righteousness arrays us in royalty as we wear it with regal confidence. "The bride, a princess, waits within her chamber, dressed in a gown woven with gold. In her beautiful robes, she is led to the king, accompanied by her bridesmaids. What a joyful, enthusiastic procession as they enter the king's palace!" (Psalm 45:13-15)

Have you dressed in your royal robes this morning so that you promenade in the world with Easter victory? When you wear them, the world will notice. By putting on your new identity as a beloved bride, you sparkle in the light of His love.

My One Gift Is You

I treasure all the many gifts
that you have given me
But ask for your remembrance
in prayer occasionally
Because it means you think enough
to ask the Lord above
To do some special favor for
someone you feel you love
And, Darling, I have faith in you
and need you by my side
Because along life's many paths
we both must need a guide
There always is that added strength
because I love you so
You are the one thing good in life
and that I'll ever know
So be my inspiration and
a better man I'll be
And soon you'll find the truth as I
that you were meant for me.

JW

The LORD says, "I will rescue those who love Me. I will protect those who trust in My name. When they call on Me, I will answer; I will be with them in trouble. I will rescue them and honor them. I will satisfy them with a long life and give them My salvation."
⌒Psalm 91:14, 16⌒

*T*he source of my father's love is our heavenly Father, who is the giver of "every good and perfect gift" (James 1:17a NIV). He treasured the gifts my mother's love had brought to him, recognizing they came from Him. She was his gift, not by what she did for him, but by simply being herself.

Our heavenly Bridegroom wants us to know we are a gift to Him. He desires us to love Him and appreciate His protection and answers to our prayers. What an abundance He is waiting to bestow on those who fear Him. "The Lord delights in those who fear Him, who put their hope in His unfailing love." (Psalm 147:11 NIV)

How wise to build a love relationship on the One who thought it up in the first place. Dad asked Mom to pray for him. He knew that if their love were to last, it would need to be based on the Lord's love for them. "By wisdom a house is built, and through understanding it is established; through knowledge its rooms are filled with rare and beautiful treasures." (Proverbs 24:3-4 NIV)

As you build your relationship with an earthly love or with Jesus, remember you are a gift that God delights in. When we love, trust and honor our Bridegroom, we give ourselves as a gift to Him. He has already given Himself to us. "Thanks be to God for His indescribable gift!" (2 Corinthians 9:15 NIV)

I Need You

You are the needed someone
on whom I can depend
To help me reach my highest goals
and all my troubles mend
You're always standing by my side
and pull me through my strife
You have become the greatest thing to enter in my life
You're something that belongs to me
and stand as my ideal
Never are you artificial
or intentionally unreal
But simply try to be yourself
in everything you do
Confirms that feeling in my heart
that I'm in love with you.

JW
⇒ No date ⇐

But now, O Israel, the LORD who created you says: "Do not be afraid, for I have ransomed you. I have called you by name; you are Mine. Others died that you might live. I traded their lives for yours because you are precious to Me. You are honored, and I love you."

*Y*ou are uniquely loved by your Creator and Bridegroom. He doesn't want you to be like anyone else, but to be yourself. My father's declaration of dependence upon his lover is a beautiful picture of intimate partnership. In the presence of such love, there is freedom to be real and vulnerable. How much more did our Bridegroom declare His love: "For you know that it was not with perishable things such as silver or gold that you were redeemed from the empty way of life handed down to you from your forefathers, but with the precious blood of Christ, a lamb without blemish or defect." (1 Peter 1:18-19 NIV)

The price for which He redeemed you confirms your value. You belong to Him now. Recognize that our Father doesn't need us, but He has chosen to desire us as His beloved sons and daughters who have the ability to bring joy to His heart. As we revel in this truth, we can't help but reflect it to the world around us. "'But you are My witnesses, O Israel!' says the Lord. 'And you are My servant. You have been chosen to know Me, believe in Me, and understand that I alone am God. There is no other God; there never has been and never will be.'" (Isaiah 43:10)

God chose Israel as a nation to declare His glory, and he chooses us as individuals to reflect His glory. Tell God of your love and gratitude for His loving you enough to invite you into an intimate partnership with Him. And while you're at it, tell Him you need Him as well!

I Want To Be A Friend Too

If the time should ever come
that you should leave me, Dear
Never more to share my love
that held me through the years
Nothing would be left for me
no love that I could hold
All would be a darkness that
the sun could not unfold
You've given me guidance
and always understood
The many things that I enjoyed
as no one but you could
And all the love for you I had
that ever filled my heart
Would still remain within me, Dear
if we should ever part
So, my Darling, I confess
and tell you in my way
That I'll love you more and more
on every passing day.

JW
April 6, 1948

*How sweet is your love, My treasure, My bride! How much better it is
than wine! Your perfume is more fragrant than the richest of spices.*
⌒Song of Songs 4:10⌒

As my father began his relationship with my mother, he
recognized a kindred spirit. He desired her friendship
and companionship as well as a romantic relationship.
They shared their dreams and desires for the future. He
depended upon her counsel and understanding heart.

Our heavenly Bridegroom also desires our intimate partnership. The
bride realizes His longing to be with her and share His life with her.
She is overwhelmed by His desire for her alone.

I would love to have seen my mother's face when she read these love
poems, or better yet, to hear her heart beating faster. Possibly her
response was similar to the beloved Shulamite in the Song of Songs
who responds, "His mouth is altogether sweet; He is lovely in every
way. Such, O women of Jerusalem, is my lover, my friend." (Song of
Songs 5:16).

All through their marriage, Mom and Dad modeled an intimate friendship. It's one of the things I admired most in their relationship. Do you
have a friendship with your heavenly Bridegroom?

You can develop your friendship with Him through seeking His guidance, enjoying His presence, appreciating His character, and joining
Him in His purposes every moment of your life.

Most of All

Though hard sometimes to realize
success is only due
In wanting something very much
my every want is you
The pattern of this world would be
a problem solved for me
If only someday you'd consent
forever mine to be
There's no forgetting your embrace
I live from day to day
To only hear you whisper that
you miss me in some way
Though love is something I'll confess
that only time will prove
In your heart and mind I hope
that doubt I can remove
Whatever glory I may find
if fortune shines on me
It will only come because
a twosome we will be.

JW
July 8, 1948

Father, I want these whom You've given Me to be with Me, so they can
see My glory. You gave Me the glory because You loved Me even before
the world began! O righteous Father, the world doesn't know You,
but I do; and these disciples know You sent Me. And I have revealed
You to them and will keep on revealing You. I will do this so that
Your love for Me may be in them and I in them.
John 17:24-26

My dad expresses his passionate love for Mom by summarizing his desire for their relationship that they would be a "twosome" never more alone. We all long to be connected with our eternal Father, the source of all love, who revealed His glory through His precious Son, Jesus.

Jesus is expressing His most important desire to His Father before His death—to purchase His beloved bride through His death. Nothing matters more to Him than this intimate love in which He desires all of us to partake.

Jesus said while here on earth, "For it is My Father's will that all who see His Son and believe in Him should have eternal life—that I should raise them at the last day." (John 6:40)

He and His Father are one in their desire for eternal relationship with each one of us. This, most of all, is Their heart for you—to be united eternally with Jesus, our Bridegroom.

Confession

Darling, I have waited long
as anyone could do
To openly confess my love
that fills my heart for you
If there is any hope for me
or measure of success
It will only come because
with you I have been blessed
To think that I could stand alone
without your fond caress
Is a thought so far from me
a fool could but possess
I've placed you on a pedestal
high above the earth
And only I can see you there
for everything you're worth
You make the darkest skies above
a glaring ray of light
That shines and spreads its warmth on me
As any summer's night
And all the things I ever do
on every passing day
Can only make me happy if
they please you in some way

JW
August 1948

A wife of noble character who can find? She is worth far more than rubies. Her husband has full confidence in her and lacks nothing of value.

Proverbs 31:10-11 NIV

On a trip to Israel, I learned how valuable rubies are. Far above my price range, I sadly declined the offer to buy some of these sparkling gems. With regret, I thought about them, wishing I could purchase them.

Our heavenly Bridegroom knows our desires. Just as my father demonstrated his love with poetry, Jesus demonstrates His love in special ways. A dear friend came to visit me one evening with a beautiful box. Her first words were, "Jesus told me to buy these for you." I could hardly wait to find out what it was!

To my amazement, the package contained a delicate set of ruby earrings. Not just single rubies, but six in each earring; twelve in total! The significance overwhelmed me as I grasped in a small way the intimate love of my Bridegroom.

It was as if He were preparing me for His future kingdom when the Holy Spirit reminded me of Revelation 21:9b-14: "Come with me! I will show you the bride, the wife of the Lamb. So He took me in the spirit to a great, high mountain, and He showed me the holy city, Jerusalem, descending out of heaven from God. It was filled with the glory of God and sparkled like a precious gem, crystal clear like jasper. Its walls were broad and high, with twelve gates guarded by twelve angels. And the names of the twelve tribes of Israel were written on the gates. There were three gates on each side— east, north, south, and west. The wall of the city had twelve foundation stones, and on them were written the names of the twelve apostles of the Lamb."

My Bridegroom had presented me with twelve jewels of His intimate love. What jewels have you received from Him?

A Birthday Wish

I search for things to tell you
on this a special day
Or adjectives quite nice enough
expressed in some sweet way
But it's hard to glorify
a star as bright as you
And many things I'd like to say
would not suffice or do
The years have made you lovelier
and nature's little feat
Was to show me you're the cause
for my heart's every beat
That I am here to serve you
and on this day each year
Just as any other day
I'll always love you, Dear

JW
1948

Then one of the seven angels who held the seven bowls containing the
seven last plagues came and said to me, "Come with me! I will show
you the bride, the wife of the Lamb." So He took me in the spirit to
a great, high mountain, and He showed me the holy city, Jerusalem,
descending out of heaven from God. It was filled with the glory of God
and sparkled like a precious gem, crystal clear like jasper. Its walls
were broad and high, with twelve gates guarded by twelve angels.
⁀Revelation 21:9-11⁀

*M*y father had trouble describing the beauty he saw in my mother. "A star as bright as you…" captures the intensity of his attraction to her. In a similar way, we, as the bride of Jesus Christ, the Lamb of God, brightly reflect His glory.

The glory of the New Jerusalem depicts our eternal glory with our Bridegroom. Her splendor is unsurpassed as she stands in glorious radiance "like a beautiful bride prepared for her husband." (Revelation 21:2) It will be an awesome sight when we are presented to our eternal Bridegroom. "Let us be glad and rejoice and honor Him. For the time has come for the wedding feast of the Lamb, and His bride has prepared herself. She is permitted to wear the finest white linen." (Revelation 19:7-8)

Now is the time of preparation for the bride. Until the day we are united with Him, we are the temple of God as the Spirit of God dwells in us and shines His light through us. One day when we are united with our Savior for all eternity, He will shine forth in His full majesty. "No temple could be seen in the city, for the Lord God Almighty and the Lamb are its temple. And the city has no need of sun or moon, for the glory of God illuminates the city, and the Lamb is its light." (Revelation 21:22-23)

Dad wanted to serve his bride-to-be every day as he waited for their marriage. Our Bridegroom serves us everyday as "He lives forever to plead with God on our behalf." (Hebrews 7:25b). Before the throne of God, He represents us as our High Priest and Lover, interceding for our every need.

His prayer for you is that He, alone, "the Bright and Morning Star" (Revelation 22:16b), would light up your life to glorify Him every day.

On Each Successive Day

The sun that rises indicates
another day is here
But the sunshine in my life
is when you're with me, Dear
You exile all my troubles and
my weakness overcome
While furnishing me strength I need
to measure up to some
We have a perfect romance and
the art of happiness
My heart rejoices only when
my arms but you possess
You're wonderful as any song
or words I could create
The strength of love has bound me firm
to you my loving mate
And because I love you so
I'll always find some way
To show you that my love will grow
on each successive day.
Jack

JW
September 20, 1948

The unfailing love of the LORD never ends! By His mercies we have been kept from complete destruction. Great is His faithfulness; His mercies begin afresh each day. I say to myself, "The Lord is my inheritance; therefore, I will hope in Him."
Lamentations 3:22-24

How tenderly my father reminds my mother that she is the "sunshine in his life." As their relationship developed and eventually they were married, this truth shone brightly. Mom had a bright, optimistic approach to life. She often encouraged Dad when he was facing pressures. Her love and presence were the wind in his sails.

Can you grasp the wonderful fact that you bring joy to Jesus' heart? Each new day, when the sun rises, there is fresh evidence of our heavenly Bridegroom's love for us. All of creation declares His love and faithfulness. "In the heavens He has pitched a tent for the sun, which is like a bridegroom coming forth from his pavilion, like a champion rejoicing to run his course." (Psalm 19:4b-5 NIV)

Your Bridegroom comes forth to bless you with His strength and fresh hope. Each new day brings with it fresh opportunity to receive His love that is completely secure regardless of life's circumstances.

Is there a situation in your life that seems hopeless? Meditate on your heavenly Bridegroom's power to help you as the sun rises on another day.

Thanksgiving Day

There is no time more opportune
than this Thanksgiving Day
To tell you that I love you, Dear
in many different ways
I thank you Sweetheart of my dreams
for making them come true
Because the only living dream
I ever had is you
You fill my heart with happiness
and by this simple phrase
I mean that you'll continue to
in all my coming days
You'll fill my heart with love and warmth
no vacancies there'll be
In my abode of happiness
as long as you're with me
So, Darling, I can give my thanks
to you and God above
For working hand in hand to bring
this gift to me of love.

JW

On the night when He was betrayed, the Lord Jesus took a loaf of bread, and when He had given thanks, He broke it and said, "This is My body, which is given for you. Do this in remembrance of Me." In the same way, He took the cup of wine after supper, saying, "This cup is the new covenant between God and you, sealed by the shedding of My blood. Do this in remembrance of Me as often as you drink it."

1 Corinthians 11:23b-25

Our Lord Jesus celebrated Thanksgiving on the night He fully gave Himself for His bride. He came into the world for one reason—to purchase His bride. A bride consisting of men, women and children from every tribe, tongue and nation. Giving Himself completely as the sacrificial Lamb of God sealed His covenant of love. And so we see Him giving thanks because He's looking ahead to the future He'll spend with His beloved bride.

Human love, as my father demonstrates, is a dim reflection of this covenant love. As Dad expresses, "the only living dream I ever had is you...you fill my heart with happiness," you can imagine the desire he had for the culmination of their love in marriage. One day their dreams did come to fruition and now my father is thanking God and my mother for 50 beautiful years together.

Soon our Savior and Bridegroom's dreams will be fulfilled when He is united with His bride for all eternity to rule and reign with Him forever.

Why don't you pour out your thanksgiving and praise to Him for choosing you to be His bride?

"You are my God, and I will praise You! You are my God, and I will exalt You!" (Psalm 118:28)

A Birthday Celebration

Your Birthday

Another year has passed for you
but only time grew old
The loveliness that you possess
is there, yet to behold
The angels waved their
magic wand
the day that you were born
And gave us something
here on earth
as bright as any morn
But I am just the lucky one
and never will be blue
Because you are the nicest thing
that I am subject to
You're all made up of sugar
a little touch of spice
A multitude of other things
that makes you awful nice
So as the years go one by one
wherever you may be
I hope that I'll be there to share
your love that's meant for me.
Jack

JW
1948

My Birthday

My birthday is a day I always
look upon with joy
And remember all the happy days
I spent when just a boy
But more because I've added
a year upon my life
A year not filled with sorrow
unhappiness nor strife
And memories of all the days
that I have spent with you
Days that I would like
to hold and
still look forward to
Because you've made
my life complete
and bright as any star
Because I long to have the type
of girl you really are
And if I always have you, Dear
to guide me 'til the last
I know my future will unfold
more promise than the past
And because it is
my birthday, Dear
I know that you'll not miss
A little hug . . . a little squeeze
And on top of that . . . a kiss.
Jack

JW
1949

You made all the delicate, inner parts of my body and knit me together
in my mother's womb. You watched me as I was being formed in utter
seclusion, as I was woven together in the dark of the womb. You saw
me before I was born. Every day of my life was recorded in Your book.
Every moment was laid out before a single day had passed.
⌒Psalm 139, 13, 15-16⌒

Your Creator dreamed you up. He uniquely fashioned you and formed you with exquisite detail. The day you were born, the angels watched in amazement at the Father's miracle. As your story unfolds, it may bring earthly love and praise as my father gives. Or, perhaps you have no one to applaud your birthday or recognize the treasure of your life. But rejoice in knowing there is one who holds you in the palm of His hand—in fact, He has inscribed your name "on the palm of His hands." (Isaiah 49:15-16 NIV)

You are His signature item—even in those times when you may feel unwanted or unloved. "When you were born, no one cared about you. Your umbilical cord was left uncut, and you were never washed, rubbed with salt, and dressed in warm clothing. No one had the slightest interest in you; no one pitied you or cared for you. On the day you were born, you were dumped in a field and left to die, unwanted. But I came by and saw you there, helplessly kicking about in your own blood. As you lay there, I said, 'Live!' And I helped you to thrive like a plant in the field. You grew up and became a beautiful jewel. Your breasts became full, and your hair grew, though you were still naked. And when I passed by and saw you again, you were old enough to be married. So I wrapped my cloak around you to cover your nakedness and declared my marriage vows. I made a covenant with you, says the Sovereign LORD, and you became mine!" (Ezekiel 16:4-8) Now that, dear one, is reason to celebrate!

Your eternal Bridegroom celebrates His earthly birthday when He entered the stream of human history to win you for His bride. Are you celebrating with Him?

This Thing Love

If I could have but just one wish
most certain I would use
My power to possess you, Dear
what better could I choose
Because you mean so much to me
but in a special way
I always seem to capitalize
on everything you say
I know you only try to help
me formulate a plan
So I can do the most for us
the way you felt I can
But, Darling, I would always try
to give you all those things
Because I know my love for you
and happiness it brings
So always give me credit for
and understanding of
The many things that go to make
the thing we know as love.

JW
March 1949

Love is patient and kind, Love is not jealous or boastful or proud or rude. Love does not demand its own way. Love is not irritable, and it keeps no record of when it has been wronged. It is never glad about injustice but rejoices whenever the truth wins out. Love never gives up, never loses faith, is always hopeful, and endures through every circumstance.
1 Corinthians 13:4-8

*W*hat a precious wish my father had for the one who had won his heart! He longed for her to embrace his love, to count on it, to know that his love for her was the source of all he did for her.

"This thing love" is the most powerful force in our lives. Our greatest need is to love and be loved. Paul described it in 1 Corinthians 13:1 as "the most excellent way." (NIV)

As Mom and Dad's love grew in their marriage, it was tested. The pressures of life can squeeze love to the limit. I can remember the day Dad came home from work, and slipped on "LaVerne Kay" shampoo streaming down the driveway. The A.M. Beauty Supply business was being started in our garage with barrels of new shampoo named after Mom. Somehow it had broken free and he almost broke his back. I must say, though, it was hilarious seeing him covered with shampoo. Dad didn't always exemplify 1 Corinthians 13—he lost his cool. But "love also covers over all wrongs." (Proverbs 10:12b NIV)

Love is not merely an emotional experience, but a choice—flowing from an unconditional source of love. As Jesus dwells in our hearts and we grasp the depth of His love for us, it will flow out to others.

I'll Always Feel the Same

It's hard for me to understand
that anyone but you
Could ever mean as much to me
the way you seem to do
It makes no difference what you wear
or what you have to say
My love is always with you, Dear
on every single day
I'm always looking forward to
the time that you will be
In my arms and whispering
that you're in love with me
I cannot be without you and
the minute we're apart
I have nothing but my love
for you that's in my heart
But if I only knew the way
you feel about me, too
It could make me very glad
or make my life so blue
Only time will answer all
the things I'd like to know
But all the while my love for you
day by day will grow.

JW

*"In that coming day," says the LORD, "you will call Me 'my Husband'
instead of 'my Master.'" . . . I will make you My wife forever, showing
you righteousness and justice, unfailing love and compassion. I
will be faithful to you and make you Mine, and you will finally
know Me as LORD.*

Hosea 2:16, 19-20

*M*y father expresses, "it makes no difference what you wear…or what you have to say…my love is always with you, Dear." Imagine if my mother had rejected his love. Our hearts cannot conceive the broken heart of God when we sin and violate His covenant love. The amazing thing is that no matter how far we've strayed, God is willing to forgive us and restore us to intimacy with Him.

Hosea displays something so intimate about our holy Bridegroom: He forgives and takes Gomer back after she abandoned him for prostitution. Now she was destitute, dirty and guilty. But it didn't stop his love from rescuing her out of the pit of her sin. This relentless, passionate pursuit pictures our beloved Bridegroom's commitment to His bride.

Is there something you're doing that may be breaking the Father's heart? Confess it now and embrace His unchanging love.

Romancing His Bride

My father's love is a picture of the Bridegroom wooing and winning His bride's love. My mother responded by marrying her romantic lover. She never wrote poetry, but expressed her love in affection, devotion and sacrifice for 50 years.

As the bride of Jesus Christ, we have the awesome privilege of responding to our heavenly Bridegroom's love. Being a royal bride of the King of kings is more than our finite minds can conceive. As it is written, "No eye has seen, no ear has heard, and no mind has imagined what God has prepared for those who love Him." (1 Corinthians 2:9b)

There's a precious joy in responding as a bride. I have discovered that His overwhelming, unconditional, intimate love empowers me every day. Carrying this treasure in my heart has opened my eyes to new facets of who He is. One of my most significant discoveries is that just as in the Jewish wedding tradition, our heavenly Father got involved in finding a bride for his Son. After sealing the covenant, His Son goes back to his Father's home, where He will wait for the Father's appointed time to consummate the marriage. I have a mental picture of this from my brother's marriage. Dad truly helped pick his bride (It's a beautiful love story I've written about in "Chosen with a Mission," my first book).

God, the Father, sent His Son to purchase His bride and bring her back to His eternal kingdom where they will rule and reign for all eternity. Jesus came to bring us to our Father. Jesus said, "I am the way, and the truth, and the life. No one can come to the Father except through Me. If you really knew Me, you would know My Father as well." (John 14:6-7).

Jesus wants us to know His Father's love as He does. He promises us, "He who loves Me will be loved by My Father, and I too will love him and show Myself to him." (John 14:21b) Understanding the Father-heart of God has deepened my intimacy with Jesus. Our Father's heart is a giving one. He has made it a reality for us to share in the most intimate fellowship possible. Jesus' final prayer for all believers expresses this desire: "Father—that just as You are in Me and I am in You, so they will be in Us, and the world will believe You sent Me." (John 17:21) Now this is the radical "first love" that the world is longing for!

I've begun Part II with "My Father's Heart" as a tribute to both my earthly father and my heavenly Father. Dad, thank you for showing me a glimpse of my heavenly Father's love for me.

Abba, Daddy, thank you for giving me Jesus, my beloved Bridegroom, Savior, and Lord. Thank you also for giving me a "legacy of love" in my mother, who showed me Jesus' humility and love. And thank you for all the other jewels You lavish upon me so generously. May these words bring to life the desire You have for the readers to know You intimately and respond to Your love.

I pray for each dear reader "to grasp how wide and long and high and deep is the love of Christ, and to know this love that surpasses knowledge—that you may be filled to the measure of the fullness of God." (Ephesians 3:18b)

My Father's Heart

How often tears have freely flowed
From the kindness that he showed.

It seems his voice is always there
When I really need someone to care.

I smile to think of his special ways
And how he sacrificially spends his days.

A sense of humor he possesses;
It always lightens and refreshes.

His love for Mom is so rich and dear;
It grows deeper each new year.

I love to see them in their chairs,
Taking a snooze from their cares.

Loving, sharing, growing old together,
Supporting each other in stormy weather.

My father is faithful and giving;
He's made my life fuller for living.

A glimpse of my heavenly Father is he.
Oh, how I desire the world to see.

A precious friend he's come to be.
An honor to be his daughter–that's me!

Love and gratitude,
Nancy

Feb. 9, 1998

The Lord is like a father to His children, tender and compassionate to
those who fear Him
⸙ Psalm 103:13 ⸙

My father has been a lifelong lover and husband to Mom, as well as a dedicated father to six children and grandfather to twelve grandchildren. He gives us a momentary view of our eternal Lover, Bridegroom, King and Father whose faithful love will carry us all the days of our life. My mind is filled with memories of his compassion and love. Always one to bring humor to a situation, he often makes me laugh in the midst of pain and disappointment. Now, watching the steadfast love and devotion he has for Mom as she grows helpless with Alzheimer's disease, I feel an even deeper appreciation of him. He lives his vow of "til death do us part" with faithfulness and care.

Jesus Himself taught us to "honor our father and mother" (Matthew 15:4) as commanded by God. He speaks about His relationship with His Father more than any other relationship, which is evidenced by His complete submission to His Father's will.

Jesus seemed to delight in His dependence upon His Father. Besides clearly identifying Himself as one with His Father, which made Him equal to God, He said, "I tell you the truth, the Son can do nothing by Himself, He can do only what He sees His Father doing, because whatever the Father does the Son also does." (John 5:19)

They are One in purpose and desire. Just as Jesus honored His Father, the Father's passion is "that all may honor the Son just as they honor the Father. He who does not honor the Son does not honor the Father who sent Him." (John 5:23)

As we honor Jesus, we are honoring our heavenly Father as well. Take some time today to honor Jesus, the Father's gift to you, as well as your Father, who loved you enough to send His precious Son. Ask Him to show you how to honor your earthly Father with whom He also blessed you.

Legacy of Love

In my dear mother I do see
A picture of love and humility.
She has gone the way of the cross
Without considering it a loss.
Willingly she has given to me,
Poured out her life full and free.
I see Jesus' purity and grace—
His acceptance in her face.
I'm grateful for her godly life,
Lived free of worry and strife.
For she has yielded her will,
Understanding how to be still
In the Potter's tender hands—
Ready for His command.
Oh, I long to be like her,
Not letting my pride deter.
For in doing there is much gain,
Even with some temporary pain.
Blessed Lord, I praise You now
For giving me a Mom who knows how
To trust in You with all her heart,
Not wanting Your will to thwart.
And now, I pray a special blessing
For Mom who I'm addressing
As a precious daughter of the King,
To you, my love I bring.
Your Daughter, Nancy

NW
Mother's Day, May 8, 1994

Rejoice with Jerusalem! Be glad with her, all you who love her and mourn for her. Delight in Jerusalem! Drink deeply of her glory even as an infant drinks at its mother's generous breasts.

Isaiah 66:10-11

*H*ow beautiful is my mother's love—a haven of comfort and joy to my heart! Even as Mom has lost much of her ability to communicate due to Alzheimer's disease, I am strengthened by the godly life she has lived. Her love and prayers are bearing fruit that will remain. She taught me to pray and to love Jesus first. I know her glorious future, the promise of her perfect eternal body that will be united with Jesus one day. She is a reflection to me of all that is true and forever.

My heavenly Bridegroom comforts me with a motherly love. Jerusalem, His holy city, has endured much and will experience the end-time battle before our King sets up His eternal kingdom. We are told to "rejoice with Jerusalem" and to "be glad for her." How can this be when we know the struggle? As we pray for the peace of Jerusalem, we join our hearts with His future kingdom vision and find comfort and peace in the midst of temporary affliction.

"Peace and prosperity will overflow Jerusalem like a river," says the Lord. "The wealth of the nations will flow to her. Her children will be nursed at her breasts, carried in her arms, and treated with love. I will comfort you there as a child is comforted by its mother." . . . "As surely as My new heavens and earth will remain, so will you always be My people, with a name that will never disappear," says the Lord.
Isaiah 66:12-13, 22

Mystery Divine

Miracle of infinite worth,
My Savior's holy birth.

Coming from heaven above,
With the power of a holy dove.

Sent my Father's heart,
To give us all a new start.

Adoption, forgiveness, and grace
Call me to seek His face.

What a wonder to behold—
Let this magnificent truth be told.

Jesus came for us to know
We can be clean as snow,

Accepted, secure, and appointed,
With His love anointed.

May we run to His manger
And take His love to a stranger.

Oh let this mystery divine,
Flow out of me to shine!

NW
January 2, 1995

*"Don't be frightened, Mary," the angel told her, "for God has decided to
bless you! You will become pregnant and have a son, and you
are to name Him Jesus. He will be very great and will be called the Son
of the Most High. And the Lord God will give Him the throne
of his ancestor David. And He will reign over Israel forever;
His Kingdom will never end!"*

Luke 1:30-33

Ll the angels in heaven must have been peering down watching Gabriel deliver the news: "Can you believe what the Lord God is going to do? And to choose a young virgin through whom to be born! I wonder how she will respond?" They must have waited breathlessly for Mary's response, just as they may wait today for the response of every heart that encounters this mystery anew—that our Creator-God desires an intimate relationship with His created ones. It's an eternal love story born in His heart, initiated and accomplished through His loving grace in coming to earth through His precious Son Jesus.

What have you done with this good news? Tucked it away for another day? Or have you embraced your Savior as Mary did—though she may not have fully understood? "Mary responded, 'I am the Lord's servant, and I am willing to accept whatever he wants. May everything you have said come true.' And then the angel left." (Luke 1:38)

Mary has been a godly example to me of a woman who embraced all God had planned for her life. Though she became the mother of Jesus, she remained His willing servant and disciple.

Through Mary's humble submission to God's initiation, all have been given a divine personal invitation to become the bride of Jesus Christ. Join with Mary today in declaring, "My soul glorifies the Lord and my spirit rejoices in God my Savior...." (Luke 1:46b-47 NIV)

Holy High Priest

My sweet suffering servant,
The way of the cross You went.

All the time I was in mind,
Your lost sheep to find.

You were tempted in every way,
So You could sympathize today.

All my struggles You chose to embrace—
So I could approach Your throne of grace.

My brokenness and pain,
Is really of greater gain.

Because I'm nearer Your heart
And nothing can thwart

Your goal for my life,
With or without strife.

As long as I'm united with You,
In intimate communication, too,

I can glory in Your presence,
For it envelopes my essence.

Oh to be like You, Jesus!

NW
January 2, 1995

So Christ has now become the High Priest over all the good things that have come. He has entered that great, perfect sanctuary in heaven, not made by human hands and not part of this created world. Once for all time He took blood into that Most Holy Place, but not the blood of goats and calves. He took His own blood, and with it He secured our salvation forever.

⌒Hebrews 9:11-12⌒

*J*esus Christ perfectly fulfills all that the Old Testament sacrificial system pointed towards. As I've studied the tabernacle and the role of the High Priest, my love and awe for Jesus have deepened. Jesus Himself became the sacrificial Lamb placed upon the altar. "Look, the Lamb of God, who takes away the sin of the world!" (John 1:29b NIV)

Not just the whole world, but my sins were paid for, my guilt was covered, my life was purchased by His blood! Oh, praise to my Prince of Victory, who rescued me from Satan's domain and transferred me to His kingdom! I belong to Jesus. "Just think how much more the blood of Christ will purify our hearts from deeds that lead to death so that we can worship the living God. For by the power of the eternal Spirit, Christ offered Himself to God as a perfect sacrifice for our sins." (Hebrews 9:14)

We are free to glory in His grace and acceptance and live as royalty— belonging to the King, wedded to the Prince of Peace. Bow before Him in humble adoration for the price He paid to purchase us. Adore Him as your Holy High Priest, who ever lives to make intercession for you!

Crossroads

You whisper, "I am the way,
I lead you day by day."

Nearer to You I long to be,
To seek Your face that
I may see

Your love poured out at Calvary,
For me to have life abundantly.

I bow low before Your cross,
Counting all else but loss.

Only to know my love,
Filled with His holy dove.

To be nearer to Your heart
Nothing in me to thwart

The flow of Your Spirit's will;
I wait yielded and still.

I ask You to take my hand,
That by Your side I may stand.

Expectant and eager to be filled,
With a heart that is stilled

I rejoice in Your embrace,
And gladly receive Your grace.

Teach me to love the cross,
Burning away sin's dross.

Yielded and moldable as clay,
Allowing You to have
Your way.

At the cross, at the cross I'll stay,
For this is where I'll find my way.

Holy Lamb, most dear,
Make my eyes clear!

Your Expectant Bride, Nancy

NW
Canada, June 1, 1995

"For I know the plans I have for you," says the Lord. "They are plans for good and not for disaster, to give you a future and a hope. In those days when you pray, I will listen. If you look for Me in earnest, you will find Me when you seek Me."

Jeremiah 29:11-13

Confused and searching for direction, trying to figure out my life, I called out to God, "Help Lord! I am sinking in a downward spiral of introspection and despair."

He heard the cry of my heart and rescued me, just like a Savior would do. "I waited patiently for the LORD to help me, and He turned to me and heard my cry. He lifted me out of the pit of despair, out of the mud and the mire. He set my feet on solid ground and steadied me as I walked along. He has given me a new song to sing, a hymn of praise to our God. Many will see what He has done and be astounded. They will put their trust in the LORD." (Psalm 40:1-3)

The crossroads in my life had to do with trust. I had to learn to depend upon Him in a deeper way. His promise to reveal Himself to me became my anchor. I realized He didn't expect me to figure things out. He already knew my future; He only wanted me to seek Him.

Are you at a crossroads in your life? It may involve your future, your faith, or facing your fears. Whatever your crossroads, seek Him first, and put your trust in Him to lead you.

New Vistas of You

My Beloved whispered in my ear,
His tender voice I'm learning to hear.

Beauty you will see today;
It's My creation on display.

I want to show you more
Of all the wonder in store.

As you seek for Me alone,
This and more you'll be shown.

For this is only a preview
Of making all things new.

There are hidden treasures also
On the path that you will go.

My Spirit illumines your night
With a new glorious sight.

My Lord Jesus, I want to be ready for the marriage supper. May
I prepare my body, soul and spirit. May your heart and life become
mine increasingly. I want to share your innermost concerns.

NW
Switzerland, June 14, 1995

Ah, Sovereign LORD, You have made the heavens and the earth by Your great power and outstretched arm. Nothing is too hard for You.
⌒Jeremiah 32:17 NIV⌒

This is what the LORD says, He who made the earth, the LORD who formed it and established it—the LORD is His name. "Call to Me and I will answer you and tell you great and unsearchable things you do not know."
⌒Jeremiah 33: 2-3 NIV⌒

Gazing at the majestic, snow-capped mountains, flowing waterfalls, lush green hillsides and radiant blooming flowers of Switzerland stirred my heart to praise. Switzerland captures the creative exuberance of our Majestic Designer. It was as if my Lover and Lord took me by the hand to show me His grandeur! His gentle whisper took my breath away. I whispered back, "Yes, Lord, I want more of You. I desire to see Your beauty, power, and great unsearchable truths!"

Isn't this the way a new bride is on her honeymoon? The bride is so eager to learn all she can about her beloved—the many facets of his personality and his physical being. It's an exciting time of discovery and fascination. First love for Jesus can be that way too!

You may want to join me in praying, "Holy Spirit, continue to give me a sense of wonder and a greater knowledge of You as I contemplate Your creation. Reveal new mysteries and facets of Your character. Open my eyes to behold You in all Your glory!"

Eternity in My Heart

Lord Jesus, I humbly receive
More than my mind can conceive.

For Your plan goes beyond time—
I hear a heavenly chime;

Eternity rings softly in my heart
Where You will never depart.

Your face will shine like the sun;
All earthly trials will be done.

What glory awaits Your bride,
To forever remain at Your side.

It's Your glory I proclaim
Without any fear or shame.

For my destiny is secure,
Away from Satan's lure.

The choice has been made—
Earthly glory will soon fade.

Jesus alone will shine;
With Him I'll forever dine.

NW
Germany, June 10, 1995

Furthermore, because of Christ, we have received an inheritance from
God, for He chose us from the beginning, and all things happen just
as He decided long ago. God's purpose was that we who were the first to
trust in Christ should praise our glorious God. And now you also have
heard the truth, the Good News that God saves you. And when
you believed in Christ, He identified you as His own by giving you
the Holy Spirit, whom He promised long ago. The Spirit is God's
guarantee that He will give us everything He promised and that He
has purchased us to be His own people. This is just one more reason
for us to praise our glorious God.
⌒Ephesians 1:11-14⌒

As a little girl, I always knew the future held the promise of something spectacular. I wondered about the beginning of time, sometimes to the point of frustration. I would take long walks in the woods trying to figure it all out. Not until I met Jesus Christ personally did it all make sense. Even my unanswered questions can now rest in peace with the one who runs the universe. For one day my destiny will be fulfilled. The purpose for which I was created will be fully realized.

Revel in being God's possession. A true bridegroom cherishes his bride as his very own. Just as a bride takes on her husband's name, we now belong to our eternal Bridegroom. We can carry eternity in our hearts until we see Him face to face and our marriage covenant is consummated in heaven.

Rejoice in your eternal inheritance!

Easter Glory

Lord Jesus,

How can I express
my love to You?
The one to whom
all honor is due?

You came to earth for my sake,
No honor of Your own to take.

Only to die a
cruel death on a cross—
What seemed like an
incredible loss.

But sin could not defeat You—
Resurrection power broke through!

You arose full of glory
To begin a brand new story;

What a precious Savior
I bow to humbly adore.

You alone deserve my all;
I gladly respond to Your call.

To forsake all and follow You—
The one to whom all praise is due.

My heart and life seem so small,
But I want to give it all.

Oh captivate my whole being,
That with new sight I'm seeing

The Holy one enthroned on high.
For You, my flesh I crucify!

Oh Beautiful Creator, King,
My soul and spirit does sing.

Sound it far and wide,
"I'm Your beloved bride!"

Loving You, Jesus,
Nancy

NW
April 16, 1995

Bless the LORD God, the God of Israel, Who alone does such wonderful things. Bless His glorious name forever! Let the whole earth be filled with His glory. Amen and amen!
⌒Psalm 72:18-19⌒

*I*t was Good Friday 1999; I was in Jerusalem basking in my Savior's love and sacrifice as I entered the gate near the mosque where devout Muslims answer their prayer call. Surrounded by God-fearing Muslims, I was startled as I heard someone cry, "Jesus!" For a fleeting moment, my thoughts drifted back in time—I visualized Jesus making His way to Calvary along the Via Dolorosa wearing a crown of thorns—His body racked with pain as He carried His cross through the narrow winding streets, accompanied by crowds of curious shopkeepers, jeering on-lookers, and wailing women.

My mind quickly returned to the present and I realized I was standing directly behind Jesus in a reenactment processional that would allow me to follow in His footsteps for the next three hours. The blood on His robes seemed all too real. All of a sudden an overwhelming sense of gratitude gripped my heart as I began to grasp the reality of just how much suffering and shame this gentle, loving Savior—the King of Glory—was willing to endure to secure a place in heaven for me. This scene is permanently imprinted on my mind and heart as I contemplate a lost world searching for answers. My hope is born anew each time I recall the wonder of that Easter morning not so long ago.

Running to the tomb two days later, not to miss the splendor of the Easter sunrise service, I felt exhilaration as never before! "He arose!" Oh, what a glorious ending—or should I say a glorious new beginning—for those of us who believe. Our painful cries are only temporary sighs. Yes, we may fail, but His victory is complete. A look at His cross and resurrection restores our hope and strength.

"Whom have I in heaven but You? I desire You more than anything on earth. My health may fail, and my spirit may grow weak, but God remains the strength of my heart; He is mine forever." (Psalm 73:25-26) Allow the glory of Easter to strengthen your heart today!

My Pledge of Love

"My Beloved is mine
and I am His;"
The beauty of His love
captivates me.

His Banner over me is
love and grace.
As I seek Him and
His lovely face,

My heart does beat with joy—
Untainted by sin's alloy.

Jesus, Jesus, holy Son,
You My Prince have won.

My heart has been set free;
Now I can clearly see!

As a treasured bride
Abiding at Your side,

I pour out my desire
For more of Your fire.

I've been wholly embraced
By Your consuming grace;

You've conquered my will;
I'm surrendered and still.

Waiting and longing to be
In Your presence to fully see

Your majesty, beauty and light—
An awesome, glorious sight.

I give You myself complete;
This is abandon so sweet;

I pledge my devotion solely
To the Lamb of God
Most Holy.

Gazing at the castle ahead,
Reminds of Your blood shed.

My eyes are fixed on my destiny,
To be with You eternally.

Fill my life with Your
beauty alone,
Just as You, Jesus, came
and shone!

I renew my vows of love,
Witnessed by Your Holy Dove.

Rekindled in my zeal,
Before You alone I kneel.

Offering myself to You,
Eagerly I say, "I do."

NW
January 19, 1996

I belong to my lover, and his desire is for me. Come, my lover, let us
go to the countryside, let us spend the night in the villages. Let us
go early to the vineyards to see if the vines have budded, if their
blossoms have opened, and if the pomegranates are in bloom—there I
will give you my love. The mandrakes send out their fragrance,
and at our door is every delicacy, both new and old, that I have
stored up for you, my lover.
Song of Solomon 7:10-13 NIV

have a favorite place to go spend time alone with Jesus. It's a private wedding chapel that faces a castle. As I was reflecting on a new year, it seemed appropriate to renew my pledge of love to Jesus.

What a wonder it is that we can be certain we belong to our King. Our heavenly, holy Bridegroom assures us of His grace and acceptance in ways too numerous to count. Nothing could be more precious than knowing I belong to Jesus! He is passionate in His desire for us to enter into this awareness. It is in His full possession of us that we can respond to His lavish love.

In contemplating His full payment of my sin on the cross, I can grasp the depth and passion of His love. It awakens in me a response, "Come, my love, I long for your intimate partnership in every detail." Being His bride involves participation in His purpose in the vineyards. It is there I can demonstrate my devotion to Him. We have a hope for a future with Him that will blossom forth into eternal fruit. My pledge of love pushes my heart to new hope that is built upon past remembrances of His intimate faithfulness. Cultivate an expectant desire as you store up delicate moments with your divine Lover. You may want to establish some special places where you can be alone with Him.

Passionate Pursuit

My Love and My Lord of All
I desire to hear Your Holy Call;

To You I will gladly heed,
You alone meet every need;

With fresh resolve, I declare,
I'm yielding to our affair;

My passionate pursuit is You,
Speak the Word, and I will do;

For Your blood has been shed for me,
Through Your mercy and grace, I'm free.

What a holy occupation,
Is my life vocation;

To belong to You alone–
My heart Your royal throne;

I live to glorify Your name,
All Your fullness is mine to claim.

Lead me on, my King,
My heart and soul do sing.

NW
1997

Place me like a seal over your heart, or like a seal on your arm. For love is as strong as death, and its jealousy is as enduring as the grave. Love flashes like fire, the brightest kind of flame. Many waters cannot quench love; neither can rivers drown it. If a man tried to buy love with everything he owned, his offer would be utterly despised.

⌒Song of Songs 8:6-7⌒

*D*id you know that the Lover of your soul is a jealous lover? He passionately desires your exclusive worship. He commands us to "not worship any other god, for the Lord, whose name is Jealous, is a jealous God." (Exodus 34:14 NIV)

An intimate partnership with my Bridegroom has produced a desire for more of Him. I long to be close to His heart, with His seal of ownership with no competition for my affection and attention. A yielded heart that obeys His every prompting is my intent. Pure and holy love is like a blazing fire that can burn away the sin in our hearts!

This intimate love can be vulnerable if not guarded. The Apostle Paul warned us to beware of being pulled away from our devotion to Jesus when he said, "I am jealous for you with the jealousy of God Himself. For I promised you as a pure bride to one husband, Christ. But I fear that somehow you will be led away from your pure and simple devotion to Christ, just as Eve was deceived by the serpent." (2 Corinthians 11:2-3)

Sometimes I've found idols trying to take the place of my "first love" for Jesus. It may be a relationship that distracts me from Him, an obsession with a project, or an opportunity where I look for satisfaction and significance. Even a good thing can begin to consume my attention and focus, and soon the fire of my "first love" diffuses.

My jealous Lover pricks my heart with an awareness of the subtle deception I've fallen prey to. As I confess my wandering heart and draw near to Him, He draws near to me. (James 4:8)

Dear beloved one, what idols tend to battle for first place in your heart? Ask your divine Lover to show you any areas of vulnerability to sin. He is jealous for your love and will place you as a seal over His heart if you ask Him.

A Grateful Heart

My offering seems so small,
In answer to the Lord of all;

In humble reverential fear,
I'm in awe that You are near;

For surely my sins are great,
And can become a heavy weight;

But my humble sacrificial Lamb,
Has Himself become the needed ram;

This amazing gift is paid,
The transaction has been made;

My knees bow in gratitude and love,
Flowing from a heart set on things above;

Your bride is awaiting that day,
May it be soon, I pray.

Love,
Your Bride

NW
1997

Since we are receiving a kingdom that cannot be destroyed, let us be thankful and please God by worshiping Him with holy fear and awe.
Hebrews 12:28

How often my little world has been shaken. It's in moments of confusion and fear that my gratitude is a pleasing sacrifice to my beloved. What kind of lover abandons His beloved when she is shaken and scared? He draws near with a whisper of love to calm her fear.

Our King has promised us His kingdom—which cannot be shaken. Listen to the whisper of His word and worship Him with the sacrifice of thanksgiving. Sit, kneel and stand in reverence and awe. Our mighty King and intimate Bridegroom is a consuming fire of faithful love and purifying holiness.

Aren't you grateful His grace has blessed your life? Thank Him today and every day. The psalmist encourages us to "Enter His gates with thanksgiving and His courts with praise; give thanks to Him and praise His name." (Psalm 100:4 NIV) Thanksgiving and praise usher us into an audience with our King and Bridegroom. It takes our focus off ourselves and onto Him, the One worthy of all our attention and honor.

Developing a lifestyle of praise testifies of His faithfulness. I have found it invaluable to keep a special thanksgiving journal as a tribute to Him. What traditions are you establishing that contribute to an "attitude of gratitude?"

Come Away with Me

Come away my beloved,
I heard You say.
"I long to meet with you
in a deeper way."

My heart responded with a leap,
I knew I had an
appointment to keep;

Schedules and planning
were arranged,
So my heart and mind
could be engaged;

What a provision and pure delight
To revel in such a beautiful sight

Oh, the water and ambience
Was not by chance—

For You had planned to
bless me here,
Your gracious gifts are very dear

Rain and wind buffeted the peace,
Until the morning brought release;

Your Spirit revealed such insight,
As Your Word brought
new light;

My heart has been changed,
My life rearranged—

For I've met with my King,
Who made my heart sing.

As I go from this place,
May I reflect Your face

To those I love on earth,
And those who need new birth!

Your Beloved Bride,
Nancy

NW
St. Petersburg, FL.
February 10, 1998

My lover said to me, "Rise up, My beloved, My fair one, and come away.
For the winter is past, and the rain is over and gone. The flowers are
springing up, and the time of singing birds has come, even the cooing
of turtledoves. The fig trees are budding, and the grapevines are in
blossom. How delicious they smell! Yes, spring is here! Arise,
My beloved, My fair one, and come away."
Song of Songs 2:10-13

*T*here's nothing to compare with the voice of my Beloved. When He calls, I seek to listen attentively. A bride desires her beloved to seek her out, to initiate and invite her attention. She longs to be reassured of His affection and the pleasure of her company.

"'Arise, My darling,' My lover said to me, 'Rise up, My beloved, My fair one, and come away.'" (Song of Songs 2:10)

I sensed a personal invitation from Jesus to be with Him for an extended time. Amazingly He provided a time and place that allowed me to seek Him with no distractions. Sometimes in the busyness of life we can't see clearly. Our Bridegroom cries, "See! The winter is past;" He desires to restore our vision of His victory and cleansing in our lives. Only then can we appreciate the flowers that are appearing in our path. New spring seasons of repairing can come forth as we listen quietly. Shhhh! Our Bridegroom might also be whispering words of His soon return for His bride.

Jesus told us, "Now learn a lesson from the fig tree. When its buds become tender and its leaves begin to sprout, you know without being told that summer is near. Just so, when you see the events I've described beginning to happen, you can know His return is very near, right at the door." (Matthew 24:32-33)

Listen closely—Can you hear His call to you? "Arise, come, My darling; My beautiful one, come with Me." (Song of Songs 2:10 NIV)

My Prince and King

What joy and pure delight,
Is in my heart tonight;

To share Your intimate love,
Now and forever above;

I revel in my royalty,
A priceless responsibility;

As I embark on our journey,
Holy Spirit prepare me;

Fill my soul with fresh fire,
Consume me with desire;

For Your glory to be shown,
Illuminating Your throne;

Oh King of the Universe,
You broke the enemy's curse;

Cause the nations to see,
Jesus died to set them free!

Teach me new revelation,
Lift me to higher elevation;

As I'm lost in wonder and awe,
That I'm delivered from the law;

Grace, grace, God's grace,
Flows from Your face;

How I long to fully display,
Father's love in a deeper way;

For Jesus, my Beloved Lover,
My deliverer, Savior, and Cover;

You are my Rose of Sharon,
When I'm feeling barren;

My Lily of the Valley,
When Satan recites his tally;

The Bright Morning Star,
When hope seems so far;

My Lover is mine and I am His,
United in heart and all His;

Oh what pleasure and pain,
Is my honor to gain;

For the sake of Your name,
I'm released from all shame;

I'm dancing with joy,
That none can destroy;

All worship to You,
My devotion is due;

I bow low at Your feet—
You lift me to my seat;

In the heavenly place,
To gaze into Your face!

Oh Jesus, I won't miss,
Your intimate kiss.

Your Beloved Bride,
Nancy

NW
En route to Trinidad
March 23, 1998

Look at My servant, whom I strengthen. He is My chosen one, and I am pleased with Him. I have put My Spirit upon Him. He will reveal justice to the nations. He will be gentle—He will not shout or raise His voice in public. He will not crush those who are weak or quench the smallest hope. He will bring full justice to all who have been wronged. He will not stop until truth and righteousness prevail throughout the earth.

Isaiah 42:1-4a

A bride is one in spirit with her bridegroom. His mission and purpose become hers. Once at a wedding shower, the discussion revolved around the bride's future plans. Someone commented, "She will go into her husband's world"— inferring that she would join him in his pursuits. As I listened, a smile crossed my face as I thought of being the bride of Jesus. "I will go into my Husband's world—and He owns the whole world." It's been my joy to journey with Him in proclaiming His love and justice to the nations. As I flew to the islands of Trinidad and Tobago, His presence gripped me. My heart embraced His passion for the lost and the price He paid to purchase them.

Our mighty King marches out in victory to establish justice on earth. He awaits His bride's full partnership in His holy battle. For He sits in the place of authority at Our Father's right hand interceding for us. We are His agents on earth to preach the gospel to the ends of the earth. Going with Him is the joy of my life. He demonstrates His love for us by letting us be involved in His purposes on earth. In confident assurance, we His bride can declare, "In His law the islands will put their hope."

"Even distant lands beyond the sea will wait for His instruction." (Isaiah 42:4b)

Drawing Close In Pain

Physically drained and full of pain,
Can this be for Your glory and gain?

My beloved You are with me,
Helping my heart and mind to see;

You are my Redeemer and Defender,
I can experience Your tender love better;

As You whisper in my ear,
You show Your love so dear;

Thank you for this test of grace,
Once again to seek Your face;

I'm believing You to heal,
Since to You I am a seal
(Song of Songs 8:6)

Placed over Your heart
Nothing can ever thwart;

"I belong to my lover—
and His desire is for me."
(Song of Songs 7:10)

Eternally Yours,
Your Bride, Nancy

NW
Florence, Italy
October 9, 1998

I want to know Christ and the power of His resurrection and the fellowship of sharing in his sufferings, becoming like Him in His death, and so, somehow, to attain to the resurrection from the dead.

☞*Philippians 3:10-11 NIV*☜

To watch God perform a supernatural work in a life is always exciting especially when that life is your own. This resurrection power was evident in my life during an incredible visit to the Middle East. There were so many open doors for ministry that I got very little sleep. I felt privileged, however, to wear myself out for His Kingdom especially when I considered the sacrifices brothers and sisters in these countries make every day to serve the King of kings.

I especially remember the Muslim taxi driver who cried when I gave him a booklet about Jesus. He told me Jesus had appeared to him in a dream. What a privilege to pray with him as he received Jesus as his Lord and Savior. But as he left me at the airport, I began to feel very sick. Something seemed to overtake my body as I got weaker and sicker. All I could do was try to persevere through a full day of travel. It wasnt until I arrived in Italy to begin another mission that I realized a parasite had invaded my body.

Pauls exhortation to "Be joyful in hope, patient in affliction, faithful in prayer," (Romans 12:12 NIV) kept me going. God graciously answered prayer and healed me. Through the ordeal, I drew closer to my Beloved as I depended upon Him to sustain me. Oh what a blessing to know Him in sickness and in health, for better or for worse. He is a faithful Bridegroom, never to depart.

The Apostle Paul proclaimed, "in all these things we are more than conquerors through Him who loved us. For I am convinced that neither death nor life, neither angels nor demons, neither the present nor the future, nor any powers, neither height nor depth, nor anything else in all creation, will be able to separate us from the love of God that is in Christ Jesus our Lord. (Romans 8:37-39 NIV)

Saints will suffer! Its part of the process of being identified with our suffering Savior. Over the years, I've experienced opportunities to love Jesus in the midst of affliction. Though minor, my sufferings have been a gift to me in developing my intimacy with Him, and have proven His overwhelming victory! What suffering are you experiencing that can deepen your fellowship with Jesus? It may be physical, emotional or mental anguish.

Entrust yourself to Him the suffering Servantto strengthen and sustain you today. He wants to bring you to a new level of identification and intimacy with Himself.

Kingdom Preparation

As I listened to my king
There came a distinct ring.
It was a clarion call
To be given out to all.

Preparation is needed
His Word to be heeded
For the time is drawing near
His message is clear.

Just as John prepared the way
For the Holy, blessed day,
Mary found favor in God's sight
And carried our treasured Light.

So, too, I must obey,
And help prepare the way
For Jesus is coming to reign
His Spirit to instruct and explain.

"The Spirit and bride say 'Come.'
And let him who hears say 'Come.'
Whoever is thirsty let him come,
And whoever wishes let him take
The free gift of the water of life."
(Revelation 22:17)

May it be soon,
Lord Jesus, come soon.
We await Your glorious sight,
Our morning star, so bright,

Reign in us today
So we can show the way.

Your holy, spotless bride,
In You, we do abide.

With eager anticipation,
Nancy

NW
December 14, 1998

Build up, build up the highway! Remove the stones. Raise a banner for the nations. The LORD has made proclamation to the ends of the earth: "Say to the Daughter of Zion, 'See, your Savior comes! See, His reward is with Him, and His recompense accompanies Him.'" They will be called the Holy People, the Redeemed of the LORD; and you will be called Sought After, the City No Longer deserted.

Isaiah 62: 10-12 NIV

We are living in days of spiritual harvest. Many are sensing the Lord's strong invitation to join Him in the building of His Kingdom. There is a divine timetable to Kingdom work. When Jesus told His disciples, "…this gospel of the kingdom will be preached in the whole world as a testimony to all nations, and then the end will come." (Matthew 24:14 NIV)

In my 25 years of ministry, I've never felt such a sense of urgency. The Lord has impressed these words from Isaiah upon my heart. Even as I've recently traveled to Israel, I've experienced a hunger there for the MESSIAH.

Gates represent points of entrance, often signifying the stronghold of a city. We're told in Rev. 21:10-12 about the twelve gates of the Holy City, Jerusalem. Our King extends His welcome to all corners of the earth. The wedding supper of the Lamb will include those people from "every tribe and language and people and nation." (Revelation 5:9b NIV)

As His bride, our role in these days is to pass through the gates and prepare the way for the people. Prayer and expectancy will build up the highway. Stumbling stones are removed when we deal with sin and cling to the Rock of Ages. Then we can triumphantly raise a banner for the nations.

Proclamation has been made through the cross of Christ. As we lift up Jesus to our generation, saying, "Your Savior comes," we unite with our Holy Bridegroom wooing His bride. The nations will see His Holy people, redeemed by His sacrifice, and will seek Him!

My Majestic King

You are the King of Kings,
To You alone my heart sings;

My light and my salvation,
My joy and inspiration;

Whom shall I fear?
When my beloved is near!

You are the stronghold of my life,
In the midst of battle and strife;

Of whom shall I be afraid?
At Your feet my burdens are laid

When enemies and foes attack me,
I fix my gaze on Your victory,

Though war may break out,
I'll give a victory shout;

One thing I ask and seek,
To remain humble and meek;

That I may dwell in Your presence,
This is the eternal essence;

To gaze upon Your beautiful face,
Hidden in the secret place,
Filled with Your glory and grace

I waited for my Lord   (Psalm 27)
Your Bride,
Nancy

NW
Arrowhead Spings, California
October 20, 1998

The LORD is my light and my salvation—whom shall I fear? The LORD is the stronghold of my life—of whom shall I be afraid? When evil men advance against me to devour my flesh, when my enemies and my foes attack me, they will stumble and fall. Though an army besiege me, my heart will not fear; though war break out against me, even then will I be confident. One thing I ask of the LORD, this is what I seek: that I may dwell in the house of the LORD all the days of my life, to gaze upon the beauty of the LORD and to seek Him in His temple. For in the day of trouble He will keep me safe in His dwelling; He will hide me in the shelter of His tabernacle and set me high upon a rock. Then my head will be exalted above the enemies who surround me; at His tabernacle will I sacrifice with shouts of joy; I will sing and make music to the LORD.

Psalm 27: 1-8 NIV

I wrote this poem in the midst of battling some strongholds in my mind. I was meditating on Psalm 27, where I found the strength I needed.

David expressed the desire of my life in this victorious psalm. Placing the Lord as our stronghold subdues fleshly strongholds that have once held our hearts captive. The world, flesh and the devil will fight for control, but we can have confidence in the Lord. What one thing would you ask of the Lord? Oh, the beauty of His presence, the shelter of His protective care, the passion and depth of His love are greater than any other false god we might devote ourselves to.

Truly, this is what our hearts were made to seek—our Bridegroom is the captivating, majestic King. Whatever stronghold you may be battling, remember your victory has already been won. Stand in faith and "Wait for the Lord; be strong and take heart and wait for the Lord." (Psalm 27:14 NIV)

Leaving Israel

There's sadness in my heart,
Though we're not far apart;

Israel, the apple of your eye,
For your peace I will cry;

Treasuring new revelation,
Adds to future anticipation

For the day my King returns,
My flesh and soul yearns.

Yeshua, teach me more,
So my heart can soar.

Strip away all other sight,
That I seek you with all my might.

NW
April 12, 1999

Then I saw a new heaven and a new earth, for the old heaven and the old earth had disappeared. And the sea was also gone. And I saw the holy city, the new Jerusalem, coming down from God out of heaven like a beautiful bride prepared for her husband.

Revelation 21:1-2

There's something so wonderful about Israel. My first trip to the Holy City captivated my heart. I called it "my honeymoon with Jesus." Since then, I've had several trips, each one marked by a unique intimacy with "Yeshua."

John was given a vision of the New Jerusalem. Our new royal relationship with our King will outshine anything we've yet experienced. The longings of our heart and soul will be completely satisfied in the presence of our King: "I heard a loud shout from the throne, saying, 'Look, the home of God is now among His people! He will live with them, and they will be His people. God Himself will be with them.' He will remove all their sorrows, and there will be no more death or sorrow or crying or pain. For the old world and its evils are gone forever." (Revelation 21:3-4)

This heavenly vision can be ours as we focus our eyes on our eternal destiny. Live in the newness of this promise, as an engaged virgin awaits the day of her wedding—no longer separated nor subject to earthly pain and loss, but dwelling with her Bridegroom forever.

"And the one sitting on the throne said, 'Look, I am making all things new!'" (Revelation 21:5a)

Running With You

Blessed love so pure,
I'm drawn to Your allure;

Holy King in royal reign,
Victor over sin and pain.

For You I surrender all,
As I hear Your tender call;

Not in noisy alarm or fear,
But a quiet whisper in my ear;

Your tender love draws me,
And sets my spirit free;

You seem to speak with care,
"New things to You I declare!

What a message to embrace,
As I seek to run my race;

I will follow as You lead,
With a compelling speed;

Time is drawing near,
Create a holy fear;

To welcome my Mighty King,
This new song I'll sing;

"All hail the power of Jesus' name
Let the world know of His glory and fame!"

Your Waiting Bride,
Nancy

NW
April 15, 1999

I don't mean to say that I have already achieved these things or that I have already reached perfection! But I keep working toward that day when I will finally be all that Christ Jesus saved me for and wants me to be. No, dear brothers and sisters, I am still not all that I should be, but I am focusing all my energies on this one thing: Forgetting the past and looking forward to what lies ahead, I strain to reach the end of the race and receive the prize for which God, through Christ Jesus, is calling us up to heaven.

Philippians 3:12-14

Throughout my journey with Jesus, I've had to embrace "new seasons." As I look ahead, I'm tempted to fret or worry about the future. "Where do I fit in to Your plan?" or "Will I be put aside? I'm no longer as young as I once was."

But even today, the Holy Spirit reminded me that I am a bride, not a wife. A bride is fresh, expectant about the future, focused on her Bridegroom. She has chosen to follow Him wherever He leads. She's captivated by her Bridegroom's love and His commitment to her. She has no fear because "perfect love casts out all fear." (1 John 4:18 NIV)

She can look ahead and smile at the future because she is running with her Beloved. "She is clothed with strength and dignity, and she laughs with no fear of the future." (Proverbs 31:25) What new paths of obedience can you anticipate because your heart is fixed on your Bridegroom? Commit your future to Him as you reach forward in faith and eager anticipation. He has laid hold of you!

Yeshua, My Beloved

You alone possess my heart,
As this year begins a new start;

My jealous Lover is mine,
With Him I will dine;

A feast for body and soul,
Is such a servant role;

My Lord and King, You gave all,
An answer to the Father's call;

I cry to know Your ways,
The pursuit of all my days;

If You are pleased with me,
Favor my eyes to see;

Your glory and holy fire,
My one and only desire;

Draw me to Your rock to stand,
Waiting for Your presence so grand!

Nancy Wilson

NW
My Birthday, May 5, 1999

Lord, You have assigned me my portion and my cup; You have made my lot secure. The boundary lines have fallen for me in pleasant places; surely I have a delightful inheritance.
⌐Psalm 16:5-6 NIV⌐

I've been tempted, at times, to compare myself with others. It may be my ministry, or gifts, or my lot in life. How often I've prayed over this promise! You, Yeshua, are my portion. Take full possession of me. Remind me that You alone know my destiny. You will also maintain my lot, and make me secure.

As we contemplate our future and refocus is critical. We can call to mind all the ways our Beloved has blessed and guided us. I've found that feasting on His faithful love nourishes my soul and energizes my service. Declaring our faith can calm our emotions.

I will praise the LORD, who counsels me;
even at night my heart instructs me.
I have set the LORD always before me.
Because He is at my right hand, I will not be shaken.
Psalm 16:7-8 NIV

His love is a foundational rock on which He can build my future. "You will show me the way of life, granting me the joy of Your presence and the pleasures of living with You forever." (Psalm 16:11)

Make this your faith declaration today! It will bring you great confidence and security.

My Father and King

What is on Your heart so pure?
I long to hear Your Word so sure;

Confirm the messages You gave,
Help me to be strong and brave;

I am weak and small,
But You are strong and tall;

Tower above the fear,
Mighty King so near;

The battle has been won,
By Your precious Son;

My passion and delight,
You shine in holy light.

At You Side,
Nancy

NW
June 14, 1999

But when you pray, go away by yourself, shut the door behind you,
and pray to your Father secretly. Then your Father, who knows
all secrets, will reward you.

⌐*Matthew 6:6*⌐

*L*earning to pray has been a great adventure. In fact, I teach a seminar called "Adventures in Prayer."

Jesus, Himself, teaches us how to pray— "This, then, is how you should pray: 'Our Father in heaven, hallowed be Your name, Your kingdom come, Your will be done on earth as it is in heaven.'" (Matthew 6:9-10 NIV) He has a Kingdom agenda that we have the privilege of participating in. What comfort we find in the secret place of prayer with Him. He shares His heart with us and aligns us with His purposes.

A child isn't expected to know everything or handle adult responsibilities. As I grew into adulthood, I found that my earthly father was still there for counsel and advice. In fact, our relationship grew as we discussed needs together.

Our heavenly Father desires our fellowship also. Not only is He our Father, but He is a mighty King who rules a kingdom. I often delight in telling others, "My Father runs the universe—He can easily handle my problems!"

Are you reveling in His majesty? "For a Child is born to us, a Son is given to us. And the government will rest on His shoulders. These will be His royal titles: Wonderful Counselor, Mighty God, Everlasting Father, Prince of Peace." (Isaiah 9:6) Don't limit Him; learn to trust Him with big and small things. Ask Him for whatever is on your heart.

Prepare Ye the Way

"Behold, I send My messenger
before your face,"
Surely, He possessed Your
glory and grace

"Who will prepare Your way
before You,"
This was His holy mission to do;

"Make His paths straight!"
His holiness can't wait.

For He is coming behind me,
Holy, pure and mighty;

To baptize with the Holy Spirit
and fire,
Fulfilling His Father's desire.

To redeem and prepare His bride
Who will soon reign at His side;

The Spirit and bride
now say "Come,"
Forsake all taking away from;

This holy passion and zeal,
That beckons us to kneel;

Asking the King of Glory
to come in,
Casting away all of our sin;

Igniting us with fresh resolve,
Our fears and doubts dissolve;

He alone prepares the way
Until His final victory day;

Come Bright Morning Star!
Lead us in Your holy war.

We assemble for Your glory,
To proclaim the Gospel story;

All of heaven rejoices,
At humble, godly choices.

Make us ready!!
Keep our hearts steady.

NW
December 22, 1999

Pass through, pass through the gates! Prepare the way for the
people. Build up, build up the highway! Remove the stones.
Raise a banner for the nations.

Isaiah 62:10 NIV

hen the Lord Jesus returns to rule and reign over the earth, Israel and Jerusalem will become the most sacred spots in the world. This glorious future is proclaimed by the prophet Isaiah. In Chapter 62, the Lord—the Creator of heaven and earth—makes a proclamation. "Because I love Zion, because My heart yearns for Jerusalem, I cannot remain silent. I will not stop praying for her until her righteousness shines like the dawn, and her salvation blazes like a burning torch." (Isaiah 62:1)

The Lord makes it clear that He has a mission for His chosen people, those He created and fashioned with His own hands. As a young Christian, I realized that I could identify with Israel, since I also had been "Chosen with a Mission" (the name of my first book). The reality of this truth has gripped my life and ordered my steps.

John the Baptist prepared the way for our Savior's first entrance into the stream of human history. Our generation has the privilege of preparing the way for His second coming. As I read Isaiah 62:10, I hear the urgency in God's command: "Go out! Go out! Prepare the roadway for my people to return!" (TLB)

We are being commissioned to go forward, to prepare the way for people. Preparation involves readiness. Ready the people for Jesus' return. "Build up the highway!" He wants as many people as possible to come into His kingdom. "Remove the stones"—get rid of all hindrances through repentance and reconciliation. "Raise a banner for the nations." A standard or banner was used to declare something of importance. "The LORD has sent this message to every land: 'Tell the people of Israel, "Look, your Savior is coming. See, He brings His reward with Him as He comes."'" (Isaiah 62:11)

Have you considered your role in helping to prepare the way for Jesus' return? What stones need to be removed from your life in order to pave the Highway of Holiness for your King?

Lord of New Beginnings

I kneel before my King,
With all of heaven's chorus.
My humble voice does sing,
"Glory to my Holy Father."

My offering seems so small'
For a King so awesome;
He is the Lord of all,
Who commands creation.

I contemplate this wonder;
From His throne flashes of lightning
And sounds and peals of thunder
Lead me to reverence and awe.

Beautiful Creator of all,
My Master, Savior and Lord;
To You my heart does call,
Lead me on, oh King eternal.

Into the new millennium,
I gladly yield my all;
As I press on toward the goal
For the prize of the upward call.

Reaching forward this I do,
Forgetting what is behind,
Looking ahead at You
With eager anticipation.

Your Bride, Nancy

NW
December 31, 1999

Listen to Me, O royal daughter; take to heart what I say. Forget your people and your homeland far away. For your Royal Husband delights in your beauty; honor Him, for He is your Lord.
⌒Psalm 45:10-11⌒

*H*ave you ever heard of a Bridegroom inviting lots of friends on the honeymoon? Of course not! He desires the complete attention of His bride. They have so much to anticipate in their future together—it's all so fresh and new. The past is gone; the bride has a new life, a new husband, new dreams. "If anyone is in Christ, he is a new creation; the old has gone, the new has come." (2 Corinthians 5:17)

"LISTEN, O daughter," your Bridegroom wants to speak to you! Let go of the past. You have a completely new identity.

For many years I sought the approval of others, measuring myself by my performance and my popularity. I especially looked for my father's approval, wanting to fulfill what I thought his expectations were. Outwardly, I seemed confident, but my security was based on whether or not I succeeded in living up to my standards.

Growing in my new identity in Christ has been so freeing for me. As I contemplated my royal position that I'm a chosen bride, beautiful and desirable to Jesus, I'm free to delight in being the person He designed me to be. Every day that I choose to put on my new, beautiful robes of righteousness, I'm filled with joy. My King welcomes me into His presence, where I experience His pleasure and love.

"The bride, a princess, waits within her chamber, dressed in a gown woven with gold. In her beautiful robes, she is led to the king, accompanied by her bridesmaids. What a joyful, enthusiastic procession as they enter the king's palace!" (Psalm 45:13-15)

You now belong to the King. He greatly desires your beauty. Believe it, revel in it, embrace your royal heritage. The Majestic King wants to fill your heart with awe and wonder that you belong to Him. Worship Him as your Lord and Bridegroom in eager anticipation. Whatever the future holds, He will be with you, delighting in you, His bride.

Sacred Romance

You are my source of joy,
With each breath I employ.

No ministry success will do—
Only putting my hope in You.

Your pleasure is my delight—
The fragrance of eternal sight.

Covenant love will stand,
My care is Your command.

What security is mine
With a husband so fine!

This day is such a token
Of Your tender love spoken.

The warmth of Your embrace
As I seek to run my race.

Let me not seek earthly gain,
Exudes mercy and grace.

It is no longer I who live;
An offering I humbly give.

Body, soul and spirit for You,
Set apart Your bidding to do.

Speak the word and I'll obey;
Tell me what to do and say.

Yielded to Your will;
All else be still!

I'm Your sacred possession—
You, my holy obsession.

Your Expectant Bride,
Nancy

NW
January 25, 2000

*...for your Creator will be your husband. The LORD Almighty is
His name! He is your Redeemer, the Holy One of Israel, the
God of all the earth.*

⌒*Isaiah 54:5*⌒

A husband means so many things. He is a protector, provider, lover, friend, partner, and confidant. Observing my Mom and Dad over the years gave me a beautiful picture of a partnership rooted in love. But the most intimate aspect of marriage is the complete oneness that the two people share. Never having been married, I can't fully comprehend this mystery, "For this reason a man will leave his father and mother and be united to his wife, and the two will become one flesh." (Ephesians 5:31 NIV) No longer two separate lives, but one! Only the Lord can bring this about.

Whether married or single, another mystery is ours to discover. And I'll never get over the wonder of this miracle—I am one with Jesus Christ. As a bride, I earnestly and passionately desire to be fully united to Jesus. Romance is kindled through sacrificial love. Eagerly saying "YES" to Jesus through obedience to His Word and the prompting of His Holy Spirit, deepens our bond of intimacy.

Sometimes, through my tears, I've knelt beside my bed to surrender to His will. Whether it be an unfulfilled desire, a relationship, or an attitude I need to embrace, I symbolically lift my open hands to Him—letting go of my will to receive His. There's a special joy in relinquishment because it releases us to receive from Him.

In marriage, two people give themselves to one another "to have and to hold from this day forward." It is a sacred covenant never to be broken. However, a good marriage just doesn't happen—it must be nourished and protected. This involves both time and effort. Have you jealously guarded your relationship with Jesus in the same way? Take time to contemplate your covenant with your beloved Bridegroom—consider ways "to have and to hold" Him more resolutely.

My Sacrificial Lover

What could move You
to such extreme?
To undergo such an evil scheme?

All the forces of hell against You,
Sorrow, torture, and death, too?

You were despised and
rejected by men,
Some didn't even know You then.

Surely You took up
our infirmities—
Knowing future atrocities.

Carrying our sorrows and pain,
We were destined to gain.

The fruit of Your suffering
and shame
Would heal the crippled
and lame—

Some in body, some in soul;
You died to make us whole.

We all like sheep have
gone astray;
Each of us has turned to
his own way.

All our iniquity was laid on You,
As a sacrificial lamb they slew.

Your blood has paid
the ransom price,
Even for soldiers who
threw the dice.

Compassion flowed when
You cried,
"Father, forgive them!"
as You died.

For soon the stone was
blasted away;
It was Your resurrection day!

Shouts of victory and awe
At what the disciples saw!

My sacrificial Lover purchased
His bride,
Ever to reign at His
wounded side!

NW
Canaan, April 2, 2000

*Surely He took up our infirmities and carried our sorrows, yet we
considered Him stricken by God, smitten by Him and afflicted.
But He was pierced for our transgressions, He was crushed for
our iniquities; the punishment that brought us peace was
upon Him, and by His wounds we are healed.*

Isaiah 53:4-5 NIV

Often I find the need to go back to the cross to contemplate my Savior's sacrifice. My heart can become callous and barren without His compassionate touch. As I ponder His journey to Calvary, I stop at each place of pain and agony, remembering what it cost Him. Kneeling in the garden, sweating drops of blood, He cried out to His Father, "…not My will, but Thine be done." (Luke 22:42b KJV) I am freshly strengthened by His humility; and I surrender. "Let us fix our eyes on Jesus, the author and perfecter of our faith, who for the joy set before Him endured the cross, scorning its shame, and sat down at the right hand of the throne of God. (Hebrews 12:2 NIV)

Oh what a gaze will do! I picture myself at the foot of the cross with Mary and His disciples. My sin nailed Him to the tree—my pride, indifference, selfishness, jealousy, fear, lack of faith. The list goes on and on. Oh, but I hear the words, "It is finished."

He now sits at the right hand of His Father in glory awaiting His complete union with His purchased bride, who will rule and reign with Him for all eternity. Just as a bride focuses on her wedding day, our thoughts should revolve around our present and future position. "Since you have been raised to new life with Christ, set your sights on the realities of heaven, where Christ sits at God's right hand in the place of honor and power. Let heaven fill your thoughts. Do not think only about things down here on earth. For you died when Christ died, and your real life is hidden with Christ in God. And when Christ, who is your real life, is revealed to the whole world, you will share in all His glory." (Colossians 3:1-4)

Thank Him today for the price He paid for your hand in marriage by sacrificing yourself for His glory. Learn to hate your sin—renounce it daily, thereby living out His victory won on the cross.

Pearl of Great Price

The midnight hour is here—
A time to draw near.

Fill my lamp with holy oil,
Wearing garments without soil.

Awaiting the wedding day,
I'll follow Jesus' way.

What a glorious goal—
To prepare my soul.

Eagerly to meet Him my All;
I will hear His triumphant call.

He'll come with a shout,
There will be no doubt.

Eternally with Him I'll reign,
An everlasting love to gain.

NW
April 7, 2000

Again, the kingdom of heaven is like a merchant looking for fine pearls.
When he found one of great value, he went away and sold
everything he had and bought it.
⌒*Matthew 13:45-46 NIV*⌒

I'll never forget when mom and dad decided to sell my life insurance. It symbolized placing my security fully in the hands of my heavenly husband. I was now in the ministry and had other provisions—namely, trusting Him to provide. However, the sale resulted in some money and they wanted me to buy a ring. What a surprise blessing!

As I shopped and prayed, jewels of all color, size and shape caught my eye. Suddenly I saw "the pearl" centered in Black Hills gold. "This is it!" I cried. "The pearl of great price! (Oh, I hope the price isn't too great!)" The salesperson, Amy, was amused. "Do you know about the pearl of great price?" I asked her. She was eager to hear.

What a joy it has been to continue to use my ring to speak about Jesus and His Kingdom. It reminds me of where my treasure lies—not in earthly gain, but in eternity, where we are told to "store up…treasures in heaven where moth and rust do not destroy, and were thieves do not break in and steal. For where your treasure is, there your heart will be also." (Matthew 6:20-21 NIV).

We can learn from the ten virgins in Matthew 25:1-13. Five were foolish and five were wisely prepared with oil in their lamps. The oil of His Holy Spirit is available to each of us daily. He will sensitize our hearts and ears to hear His voice. As we respond with readiness to His prompting, we lay up spiritual treasures. Then we'll be ready for the midnight cry— "Look, the Bridegroom is coming! Come out and welcome Him!" (Matthew 25:6b)

Are you as prepared as the five wise virgins were, awaiting your Bridegroom's return? Each morning ask him to fill and empower you with His Holy Spirit. Live daily in His presence and power and lay up treasures in heaven. Your expectancy for His return will purify your heart of lesser purposes.

Waiting in Anticipation...

"The bride belongs to the Bridegroom,"
This truth dispels all fear and gloom.

There's a sense of wonder and awe;
Jesus, my Beloved, He saw.

He heard my Bridegroom's voice,
Confirming I was His choice.

Joy was His, full and complete,
For Jesus had come to meet.

"He must become greater; I must
become less;"
John's goal was not to impress.

He had fulfilled His role,
Preparing the way for each soul.

John was a lamp to give light,
Burning with eternal sight.

A forerunner to point the way
To my future wedding day.

Now I can rejoice
Since Jesus is my choice.

I am His; He is mine.
Daily with Him I dine

Awaiting the marriage feast,
Prepared for the greatest and the least.

Until then, I will fulfill my call,
Completing John's preparation for all.

The Spirit and the bride say, "Come,"
And let him who hears say, "Come!"

"Whoever is thirsty, let him come;
and whoever wishes, let him take
the free gift of the Water of Life."
(Rev. 22:17 NIV)

My fascinated heart is smitten,
Exhilarated by every Word written;

"He who testifies to these things
says, "Yes, I am coming soon.'"

Amen. Come, Lord Jesus.
The grace of the Lord Jesus be with
God's people. Amen
(Rev. 22:20-21 NIV)

I am ravished with delight,
With Your passionate love so bright.

Keep my heart on fire,
Kindled with fresh desire.

To magnify Your holy name,
Free from all condemnation and shame!

Your Purchased Bride,
Nancy

≈ NW ≈

First Love: A Devotional
Nancy Wilson

First Love captures the passion of an intimate love relationship with Jesus Christ in a unique and moving fashion. Using the poems her father wrote for her mother during their courtship over 50 years ago, Nancy creatively parallels his expression of love with the love of our heavenly Bridegroom, Jesus Christ, for His bride.

Nancy's poetry and intriguing devotionals give the reader a deeper understanding of the "bridal" love for Jesus. Her personal insights and scriptural principles will inflame your heart with a passion to respond to the Lover of your soul with fresh inspiration and commitment.
Paperback / 128p / ISBN 1-56399-156-X / 1.800.729.4351

Chosen With A Mission: Discover the Adventure
Nancy Wilson

Delightfully entertaining, practical, and inspirational, Chosen With A Mission sizzles with Nancy's real-life adventures while presenting a solid blueprint for understanding and fulfilling the unique mission God has for each of us. You will discover exciting possibilities of the Christian life from God's Word and His work in Nancy's life, such as:
- her time behind bars, experiencing the true meaning of grace
- her job as a dolphin trainer, learning that God's plan is never boring
- her battle with an eating disorder, applying God's power to over come
- her world travels, practicing evangelism as a way of life

She seasons each story with insightful truth for readers of all ages. If you are ready for the adventure, *Chosen With A Mission* is a must-read.
Paperback / 193p / ISBN 1-57902-010-0 / 1.800.729.4351

Chosen With A Mission Companion Study Guide
Nancy Wison

Ever wondered why you're here?
Want to know what it means to be chosen by God?
Do you want to know God in a deeper way?
You will be able to find answers to these questions and more as you work through the pages of this study guide. You will be challenged by thought -provoking questions, faith-strengthening truths from the Bible, and helpful encouragement for your prayer life.

Designed as a companion for Nancy Wilson's book, *Chosen With A Mission*, this study guide can be used individually or with a group. The versatile content will benefit anyone interested in learning more about what it means to be chosen by God.

Paperback / 65p / ISBN 1-57902-013-5 / 1.800.729.4351

Audio Tapes
Nancy Wilson

The King's Commission: Respond to God's challenge to be a world-changer and significantly influence your generation.

Secure With Your Singleness: Saying "yes" to the will of God can involve embracing His gift of singleness. Nancy shares her personal experience and God's perspective on the topic.

How to Be Filled With the Spirit: Learn how to experience a dynamic relationship with God through the Holy Spirit's power.

Reaching the Next Generation: A challenging look at how to be women who can influence our generation.

Prayer Is Not an Option: Learn how to tap into the King's power to make a difference in your personal prayer life.

Winning and Discipling Youth to Run God's Race: A vision-packed message filled with "how to's" for developing a ministry to youth.

In Search of the Ideal: Overcome the struggle with comparison, performance, and insecurity as Nancy explains how to replace wrong beliefs with solid truths. Nancy shares her own journey in overcoming an eating disorder.

Journey to the Heart of God: Discover timeless truths about the Father's favor, Jesus' victory and the Holy Spirit's work in your life

To order call 1.800.729.4351

Speaker
Popular speaker for middle and high school students, women, youth leaders, prayer events, and evangelistic outreaches.

She speaks on a wide variety of topics, challenging participants to passionately pursue Jesus Christ and His mission for every believer.

For further information contact Nancy Wilson
100 Lake Hart Drive, Dept. 3200
Orlando, FL 32832
phone: 407-826-2174
nwilson@studentventure.com